LIVING THE
LETTERS
Colossians

LIVING THE LETTERS
Colossians

A NavStudy Featuring

OUR GUARANTEE TO YOU

We believe so strongly in the message of our books that we are making this quality guarantee to you. If for any reason you are disappointed with the content of this book, return the title page to us with your name and address and we will refund to you the list price of the book. To help us serve you better, please briefly describe why you were disappointed. Mail your refund request to: NavPress, P.O. Box 35002, Colorado Springs, CO 80935.

The Navigators is an international Christian organization. Our mission is to advance the gospel of Jesus and His kingdom into the nations through spiritual generations of laborers living and discipling among the lost. We see a vital movement of the gospel, fueled by prevailing prayer, flowing freely through relational networks and out into the nations where workers for the kingdom are next door to everywhere.

NavPress is the publishing ministry of The Navigators. The mission of NavPress is to reach, disciple, and equip people to know Christ and make Him known by publishing life-related materials that are biblically rooted and culturally relevant. Our vision is to stimulate spiritual transformation through every product we publish.

ISBN-13: 978-1-60006-162-2
ISBN-10: 1-60006-162-1

Cover design by Disciple Design
Cover photo by Phillip Parker
Creative Team: Terry Behimer, Brad Lewis, Cara Iverson, Kathy Mosier, Arvid Wallen, Pat Reinheimer

Written and compiled by John Blase

Some of the anecdotal illustrations in this book are true to life and are included with the permission of the persons involved. All other illustrations are composites of real situations, and any resemblance to people living or dead is coincidental.

All Scripture quotations in this publication are taken from *THE MESSAGE* (MSG). Copyright © 1993, 1994, 1995, 1996, 2000, 2001, 2002, 2005. Used by permission of NavPress Publishing Group.

Printed in the United States of America

1 2 3 4 5 6 7 8 9 10 / 10 09 08 07

CONTENTS

ABOUT THE
LIVING THE LETTERS
SERIES

Letters take time to write, usually much more time
than talk. They require a certain level of artfulness and
thoughtfulness in expression. Then they remain, to be reread,
perhaps to be stored away for another day of reading, or
even to be encountered some distant time by a future,
unknown eavesdropper. All of these aspects of the letter
invite soulfulness: rereading is a form of reflective meditation;
keeping letters honors memory and not only daily living;
and speaking to a reader not yet present in this life
respects the soul's eternal nature.
—THOMAS MOORE, *SOUL MATES*

This isn't your typical Bible study. You won't find any blanks to fill in, questions with obvious answers, or maps of Paul's missionary journeys.

So what is *it?* That's a good question. Think of this book as an opportunity. It's a chance to allow God's Spirit to speak to you in a way that he's done for centuries—through letters.

Unfortunately, we live in a time when many consider e-mail a form of letter writing. Every once in a while, it might be. But usually it's not. Think about it: E-mail is often written quickly and absentmindedly. How many times have you clicked *send* and then thought, "Oh, no!"

As Moore points out in the above quote, letter writing takes time. Letter reading does too. So you can view this as an opportunity to add time to your day, or at least to spend what time you have in a worthy manner.

This collection of paper and ink takes Paul's letter to the Colossians and surrounds it with letters and journal entries from others in history who seemed to be trying to invite some of the same *reflective meditation*. Please understand that this isn't a subtle attempt to equate a letter or journal entry of Samuel Rutherford with the divinely inspired letter written by Paul. If anything, it's an attempt to underscore the timeless quality of God's correspondence with humanity—and to be aware of God speaking in a letter written by Anne Lamott or your Uncle Jasper.

Briefly, each lesson includes an entry from Paul's letter to the Colossians (using Eugene Peterson's *The Message*), followed by several other "letters" and a poem from contemporary writers. The challenge is to read and reread these letters. Come back and read them again days or weeks later. Questions and statements along the way will challenge you to engage the words on the page, prodding your heart, mind, soul, and strength. Yet don't approach any of this quickly or absentmindedly; rather, aim to live over and over again what you read and learn.

In so doing, might your life resemble something meditative, memorable, and eternal. *Live the letters.*

HOW TO APPROACH
LIVING THE LETTERS

This NavStudy is meant to be completed on your own and in a small group. You'll want to line up your reflection group (or whatever you want to call it) ahead of time. A group of four to six is optimal—any larger, and one or more members will likely be shut out of discussions. Your group can also be as small as two. Each person will need his or her own copy of this book.

Lessons follow the rhythm of *lectio divina*, the ancient practice of *divine reading*. The four movements are the ingredients of a spiritual frame of mind: (1) *Read*—the recitation of a short text of Scripture; (2) *Think*—an effort to wrestle with the meaning of a passage and make it personally relevant; (3) *Pray*—responding to the text and asking for God's grace in doing so; and (4) *Live*—experiencing God's love and his will for you. Divine reading has also been described in this way: Reading lies on the surface, thinking moves to the inner substance, praying involves voicing the desire, and living is the experience.

For each lesson in this book, use the four movements as follows:

1. *Read* the Scripture passage and the other readings in each section. Let them soak in. Saturate your heart, mind, soul, and strength. Reread if necessary. There's no blue ribbon for finishing quickly. Make notes in the white space on the page. If you like journaling, think of this as a space to journal.

2. *Think* about what you read. Take your time and respond to the questions provided. In addition to the questions, always ask, "What does this mean?" and "Why does this matter?" about the readings. Use your reflections to generate discussion with the other people in your group. Allow the experience of others to broaden your wisdom. You'll definitely be stretched—called on to evaluate what you've discovered

and asked to make practical sense of it. In community, this stretching can often be painful and sometimes even embarrassing. However, your willingness to be transparent—your openness to the possibility of personal growth—will reap great rewards.

3. *Pray.* That sounds so easy, doesn't it? But we all know it's not. In each lesson, read the poem provided and let God's Spirit cause words and phrases to stand out and be combined with the thoughts from the readings. Then allow that combination to be your prayer. It won't sound like a regular prayer; in fact, let this time expand your usual practice of prayer. At times, you might not be able to voice your thoughts aloud. Remember, the Spirit intercedes for us, interpreting even our "groans" to the Father.

4. *Live. Live* as in rhymes with *give.* How can you live out the thoughts, feelings, emotions, truths, challenges, and confessions you've experienced in the lesson? Each lesson will encourage you to write a letter to yourself. When your group gets together, talk over these letters. Commit to living out what you express in your letter, and ask your small group to hold you accountable with prayer and support.

TIPS FOR SMALL GROUPS

After going through each week's lesson on your own, sit down with a few other people and go deeper. Here are a few thoughts on how to make the most of that time.

Set ground rules. You don't need many. Here are two:

First, you'll want to commit, as a group, to see this through to completion. Significant personal growth happens when group members spend enough time together to really get to know each other. It doesn't have to be every week, but you do need to establish some element of consistency to your time together.

Second, agree together that everyone's story is important. Time is probably the most valuable commodity today, so if you have just an hour to spend together, do your best to give each person ample time to express concerns, pass along insights, and feel like a participating member of the group. Small-group discussions aren't monologues; however, a one-person-dominated discussion isn't always a bad thing either. Not only is your role in a small group to explore and expand your own understanding, it's also to support one another. If one group member truly needs more of the floor, give it to that person. There will be times when the needs of the one outweigh the needs of the many. Use good judgment and allow extra space when needed; *your* time might be the next time your group meets.

Meet regularly. Choose a time and place, and stick to it. Don't be surprised if this becomes a struggle. Go into this study with that expectation and push through it.

Let God lead. Each time you get together, guess who else is in the room? That's right—God. Be sensitive to how he is leading. Does your time need to be structured? If so, following the book's structure is a good idea. Does the time need breathing room instead? Then take a breath, step back, and see what God does.

Talk openly. You'll all be a little tentative at first. You're not a bad person if you're hesitant to unpack all your *stuff* in front of friends or new acquaintances. Maybe you're just a little skeptical about the value of revealing to others the deepest parts of who you are. Maybe you're simply too afraid of what those revelations might sound or look like. Discomfort isn't the goal; rather, the goal is a safe place to share and be. But don't neglect what brings you to this place—the desire to be known and find meaning for your life. And don't forget that God brings you to this place; you're not a part of your group by chance. Stretch yourself. Dip your feet in the water of honest discussion. Healing can often be found there.

Stay on task. Do you know what TMI is? Too much information. Don't spill unnecessary stuff. Talk-show transparency does little more than bolster ratings and reveal a lack of preparation. If structure isn't your group's strength, then try this approach: Spend a few minutes sharing general comments about the study, and then take each question and give everyone in the group a chance to respond.

While you're listening to others, write down thoughts that their words prompt within you. When you get to the Pray section, listen to each other read prayers aloud. Finally, give time to each person's Live section. What did each of you experience in writing a letter to yourself?

Follow up. Don't let the life application drift away without further action. Be accountable to each other and refer to previous lessons' Live sections often. Take time at the beginning of your group's meeting to review and see how you're doing. Pray for each other between times you get together. Call group members who God brings to your mind and simply ask, "How ya doin'?"

STALWART

"May everything good from God our Father be yours!"
(Colossians 1:2)

Before You Begin

Take just a few moments to still your heart and mind. Remember, God desires to speak to *you* in these moments.

> God *is sheer mercy and grace;*
> *not easily angered, he's rich in love.*
>
> PSALM 103:8

READ

Colossians 1:1-8

I, Paul, have been sent on special assignment by Christ as part of God's master plan. Together with my friend Timothy, I greet the Christians and stalwart followers of Christ who live in Colosse. May everything good from God our Father be yours!

Our prayers for you are always spilling over into thanksgivings. We can't quit thanking God our Father and Jesus our Messiah for you! We keep getting reports on your steady faith in Christ, our Jesus, and the love you continuously extend to all Christians. The lines of purpose in your lives never grow slack, tightly tied as they are to your future in heaven, kept taut by hope.

The Message is as true among you today as when you first heard it. It doesn't diminish or weaken over time. It's the same all over the world. The Message bears fruit and gets larger and stronger, just as it has in you. From the very first day you heard and recognized the truth of what God is doing, you've been hungry for more. It's as vigorous in you now as when you learned it from our friend and close associate Epaphras. He is one reliable worker for Christ! I could always depend on him. He's the one who told us how thoroughly love had been worked into your lives by the Spirit.

THINK   *"I took all this in and thought it through, inside and out."* (Ecclesiastes 9:1)

- Paul refers to the believers in Colosse as "stalwart," which means "strongly and stoutly built; sturdy and robust."[1] When you think about a sturdy or robust believer, who comes to mind? What is it about him or her that says "stalwart"?
- Think about the group of believers you run with. If Paul greeted your group, would he use words like "strongly and stoutly built; sturdy and robust"? If so, why? If not, what words might he use?

- Consider Paul's statement, "The lines of purpose in your lives never grow slack, tightly tied as they are to your future in heaven, kept taut by hope." Think about your own line of faith. Is it taut, slack, threadbare, or what? How do you think hope plays into the condition of your faith?

READ

From *Scott's Last Expedition* by Robert Falcon Scott[2]

Monday, January 8

(In November 1910, the vessel *Terra Nova* left New Zealand carrying a team of explorers led by Robert Falcon Scott. Scott's goal was to be the first man to reach the South Pole. He kept a detailed journal until March 29, 1912, when the last of the team was lost in a blizzard.)

It is quite impossible to speak too highly of my companions.

Each fulfills his office to the party; Wilson, first as doctor, ever on the lookout to alleviate the small pains and troubles incidental to the work; now as cook, quick, careful and dexterous, ever thinking of some fresh expedient to help the camp life; tough as steel on the traces, never wavering from start to finish.

Evans, a giant worker with a really remarkable headpiece. It is only now I realize how much has been due to him. Our ski shoes and crampons have been absolutely indispensable, and if the original ideas were not his, the details of manufacture and design and the good workmanship are his alone. . . .

Little Bowers remains a marvel—he is thoroughly enjoying himself. I leave all the provision arrangement in his hands, and at all times he knows exactly how we stand, or how each returning party should fare. . . . Nothing comes amiss to him, and no work is too hard. It is a difficulty to get him into the tent; he seems quite oblivious of the cold, and he lies coiled in his bag writing and working out sights long after the others are asleep.

Of these three it is a matter for thought and congratulation that each is specially suited for his own work, but would not be capable of doing that of the others as well as it is done. Each is invaluable.

THINK   "I took all this in and thought it through, inside and out." (Ecclesiastes 9:1)

- In Colossians 1:1, Paul says that he's on a "special assign-ment." Scott was on an expedition to the South Pole. Can you see any benefit to viewing the life of faith in these kinds of terms? Why or why not?
- A little more than two months after he wrote this journal entry, Scott and a few remaining men froze to death in a brutal blizzard. Yet his writing seems to describe vigor, vitality, and oblivion to the cold. How do you account for this?
- Have you ever experienced anything like this—an extreme sturdiness in the face of insurmountable odds? This doesn't have to be a polar expedition. It might be as mundane as surviving the holidays with your family.

READ

From *The Worst Journey in the World* by Apsley Cherry-Garrard[3]

Never Again

(Apsley Cherry-Garrard was one of Scott's expedition members. He formed a search party and eventually found the bodies of Scott and his companions, along with Scott's journal entries.)

There are many reasons which send men to the poles, and the Intellectual Force uses them all. But the desire for knowledge for its own sake is the one which really counts and there is no field for the collection of knowledge which at the present time can be compared to the Antarctic.

Exploration is the physical expression of the Intellectual Passion.

And I tell you, if you have the desire for knowledge and the power to give it physical expression, go out and explore. If you are a brave man you will do nothing: if you are fearful you may do much, for none but cowards have need to prove their bravery. Some will tell you that you are mad, and nearly all will say, 'What is the use?' For we are a nation of shopkeepers, and no shopkeeper will look at research which does not promise him a financial return within a year. And so you will sledge nearly alone, but those with whom you sledge will not be shopkeepers: that is worth a good deal. If you march your Winter Journeys you will have your reward, so long as all you want is a penguin's egg.

THINK   "I took all this in and thought it through, inside and out." (Ecclesiastes 9:1)

- Do you think believers today could be described as "shopkeepers"?
- When you think of the word *stalwart* and the idea of "strongly and stoutly built; sturdy and robust," what words or phrases in this passage mean something to you?

- Go back through the passage and substitute the word "God" for the words "knowledge" and "a penguin's egg." With these substitutions, what are your reactions to the passage? Keep in mind the word *stalwart* and its definition.

READ

From *Arctic Dreams* by Barry Lopez[4]

The Intent of Monks

(A carraugh is a long, narrow, and open but seaworthy boat consisting
of a wickerlike basket frame covered with oak-tanned ox hide
and caulked with tallow.)

In the following pages, beginning in a time before the sagas, the
notion of a road to Cathay, a Northwest Passage, emerges. The
quest for such a corridor, a path to wealth that had to be followed through a perilous landscape, gathers the dreams of several ages. Rooted in this search is one of the oldest of all human
yearnings—finding the material fortune that lies beyond human
struggle, and the peace that lies on the other side of hope. . . .

The people who first came into the Arctic had no photo-
graph of the far shore before they left. They sailed in crude ships
with cruder tools of navigation, and with maps that had no foundation or geographic authority. They shipwrecked so often that
it is difficult to find records of their deaths, because shipwreck
and death were unremarkable at the time. They received, for the
most part, no support—popular or financial. . . . Their courage
and determination in some instances were so extreme as to seem
eerie and peculiar rather than heroic. Visions of achievement
drove them on. In the worst moments they were held together
by regard for each other, by invincible bearing, or by stern naval
discipline. Whether one finds such resourceful courage among
a group of young monks on a spiritual voyage in a carraugh, or
among worldly sailors with John Davis in the sixteenth century,
or in William Parry's snug winter quarters on Melville Island in
1819–20, it is a sterling human quality.

THINK   "I took all this in and thought it through, inside and out." (Ecclesiastes 9:1)

- Compare Paul's description of the Colossian believers as having a "future in heaven, kept taut by hope" with Lopez's description of these early explorers as "finding . . . the peace that lies on the other side of hope."

- Look again at Lopez's descriptions of the explorers and the conditions they faced. Do you think any of these phrases could be used to describe the early believers in Colosse?

- What about believers today? Do you think the faith of some could be described as less "sturdy and robust" because it comes without great difficulty? Explain.

READ

From *Brendan* by Frederick Buechner[5]

The Fire in the Woods

(Buechner tells of the birth of the colorful sixth-century
Irish saint Brendan. Erc is the name of the bishop.)

Erc said the night the boy was born he saw the woods by the
boy's house catch fire. It wasn't any common kind of fire
either. . . . There was no smoke. The whole woods went up in a
single vast flame behind the house, and the color of the flame
was such a fiery gold clear through that it turned the house gold
and the eyes of Erc gold as he stood in the dark watching and
waiting with the tide scudding in among the monstrous hills
behind him. For a greater wonder still, Erc said, by the time dawn
came and the boy was fully born out into the world and wrapped
up as snug as a badger against the chill, there wasn't so much as
one dry twig blackened or the delicatest feather of a bird's wing
singed.

Finnloag was the boy's father and Cara his mother, free born
and of the new faith both of them. . . . The name they give the
boy was Brendan, and Brendan is the name he carried with him
to the grave where he's no likelier to need a name any longer if
you ask me than any of the rest of us when our time comes. Save
for life itself and a few small gifts along the way, his name was
about the only thing he had from Finnloag and Cara nearly.

THINK   "I took all this in and thought it through, inside and
            out." (Ecclesiastes 9:1)

- What are your impressions of Brendan? What one word or
  phrase would you use to describe him?
- Brendan grew up and became a legendary saint in Ireland.
  Yet, "save for life itself and a few small gifts along the way, his
  name was about the only thing he had." What do you think
  that means?

- Reread Colossians 1:1-8 at the beginning of this Letter. In addition to Timothy, Paul mentions Epaphras, whose name is mentioned in Scripture just three times (twice in Colossians and once in Philemon). Can you think of any ways Epaphras and Brendan are alike? Different? Explain.

PRAY

Slowly read the following poem a couple of times. What speaks to you? Ask God to bring a word or phrase to the surface. Then allow that word or phrase to begin your prayer. It might seem awkward at first. Fine, let it be awkward. But stick with it.

The Seven Pillars of Wisdom

All men dream: but not equally.
Those who dream by night in the dusty
recesses of their minds wake in the day
to find that it was vanity: but the dreamers
of the day are dangerous men, for they may
act their dreams with open eyes, to make it
possible.

—T. E. LAWRENCE[6]

LIVE

These words from Lawrence serve as a reminder of this section's theme—*stalwart*:

> But the dreamers
> of the day are dangerous men.

You've read from the journal entries, letters, and poems of others. Now it's your turn. What does God want you to live when it comes to *stalwart*? Use the space below to write a letter to yourself. You might want to date the letter so you can reflect later where you were and what was going on in your life regarding *stalwart*.

Date _____

Dear _____

INCARNATION

"*Everything* got started in him and finds its purpose in him."
(COLOSSIANS 1:16)

Before You Begin

Take just a few moments to still your heart and mind.
Remember, God desires to speak to *you* in these
moments.

> *Blessed be the Lord —*
> *day after day he carries us along.*
>
> PSALM 68:19

READ

Colossians 1:13-20

God rescued us from dead-end alleys and dark dungeons. He's set us up in the kingdom of the Son he loves so much, the Son who got us out of the pit we were in, got rid of the sins we were doomed to keep repeating.

We look at this Son and see the God who cannot be seen. We look at this Son and see God's original purpose in everything created. For everything, absolutely everything, above and below, visible and invisible, rank after rank after rank of angels—*everything* got started in him and finds its purpose in him. He was there before any of it came into existence and holds it all together right up to this moment. And when it comes to the church, he organizes and holds it together, like a head does a body.

He was supreme in the beginning and—leading the resurrection parade—he is supreme in the end. From beginning to end he's there, towering far above everything, everyone. So spacious is he, so roomy, that everything of God finds its proper place in him without crowding. Not only that, but all the broken and dislocated pieces of the universe—people and things, animals and atoms—get properly fixed and fit together in vibrant harmonies, all because of his death, his blood that poured down from the cross.

THINK   "I took all this in and thought it through, inside and out." (Ecclesiastes 9:1)

- Go back and circle your favorite words or phrases in this passage. Why do they have special meaning to you?
- Based on Paul's words, how would you respond to someone who said, "No one has ever seen God"?
- In general, what kind of shape do you think the church is in?

Would you describe it as on the rise, stagnant, going down-hill fast, or what? If Christ "organizes and holds" the church together, how do you account for its current condition?

READ

From *God in the Flesh* by Don Everts[1]

Fixing Our Eyes on Jesus

At the beginning of his Gospel, John writes simply and beautifully of God's strategy, "No one has ever seen God. [Thanks for rubbing it in, John!] It is God the only Son, who is close to the Father's heart, who has made him known" (John 1:18).

And this is why things got so interesting when Jesus came to earth. You see, God (the invisible God) had sent Jesus to fully reveal himself. Literally, God in the flesh. Paul reminds the Colossians that Jesus is "the image of the invisible God" (Colossians 1:15). Somehow God had actually pulled it off. He was actually able to enflesh himself in a human being.

And this wasn't a cut-rate semi-God. It's not like Jesus was some less-filling, "light" version of the Almighty. Paul assures us that *all of the fullness of God* dwelt in Jesus. And all of the fullness of God—all of it—was *pleased* to dwell in Jesus (Colossians 1:19). . . .

Jesus of Nazareth, the small-town carpenter, was the very flesh of the almighty, eternal, invisible God, Yahweh.

And as Jesus walked upon the earth, every decision he made, every lesson he taught, every conversation he had tells us about God. His posture, his manner of heart, his attitude, his outlook, his pace, his emotions, his death—all reveal God.

Every square inch of everything Jesus ever did speaks of God. His very life (not just his death) is utterly and simply sublime.

THINK   "I took all this in and thought it through, inside and out." (Ecclesiastes 9:1)

- Everts writes that "the fullness of God—all of it—was *pleased* to dwell in Jesus." Have you ever considered that before? What thoughts does it stir in you?

- "Apparently God was having a great time walking around with two feet and a head of hair." What's your reaction to the preceding sentence? Reflect on your answer.
- On the list of influencers in your life, where is Jesus? Top of the charts, high-but-not-tops, on a level with Thoreau or Shakespeare, or where? Has Jesus always held that position, or has he climbed or fell a few rungs on your ladder? Explain.

READ

From *Further Along the Road Less Traveled* by M. Scott Peck[2]

The Difference He Makes

I was absolutely thunderstruck by the extraordinary reality of the man I found in the Gospels. I discovered a man who was almost continually frustrated. His frustration leaps out of virtually every page: "What do I have to say to you? How many times do I have to say it? What do I have to do to get through to you?" I also discovered a man who was frequently sad and sometimes depressed, frequently anxious and scared. . . . A man who was terribly, terribly lonely, yet often desperately needed to be alone. I discovered a man so incredibly real that no one could have made Him up.

It occurred to me then that if the Gospel writers had been into PR and embellishment, as I had assumed, they would have created the kind of Jesus three quarters of Christians still seem to be trying to create . . . portrayed with a sweet, unending smile on His face, patting little children on the head, just strolling the earth with this unflappable, unshakable equanimity. . . . But the Jesus of the Gospels—who some suggest is the best-kept secret of Christianity—did not have much "peace of mind," as we ordinarily think of peace of mind in the world's terms, and insofar as we can be His followers, perhaps we won't either.

THINK   "I took all this in and thought it through, inside and out." (Ecclesiastes 9:1)

- How do you react to Peck's words? Agree? Disagree? Unsure?
- Peck describes Jesus as "a man who was frequently sad and sometimes depressed, frequently anxious and scared." Do you think this is too much humanity to attribute to Jesus? Explain.

- What about Peck's "peace of mind" statement—do you think he's accurately describing Jesus? Or is he reading too much of his own stuff into the person of Christ?
- Even if you don't agree with Peck's discoveries, how could Jesus end up as the "best-kept secret of Christianity"?

READ

From *Girl Meets God* by Lauren F. Winner[3]

Christmas

(Winner's book describes her pilgrimage from being an Orthodox Jew to becoming a Christian.)

Admittedly, it's a little crazy. Grand, infinite God taking on the squalling form of a human baby boy. It's what some of the old-timers call a scandal, the scandal of the Gospel. But it is also the whole point.

I've filled my bedroom with pictures of Jesus. Icons and paintings and church fans and other Jesuses dance all over my walls. Everywhere you turn, there He is, peering at you. Sometimes with a halo, sometimes on a cross, sometimes knocking at a door. When I don't much like Christianity, or when I can't remember why I am doing any of this, I look at these pictures of Jesus. Often I talk to them. I talk to them when I am too distracted, otherwise, to pray, and I talk to them when none of my friends are home and I am bored and alone. . . .

In my more pompous moments, I describe myself, my Christianity, as *radically incarnational*. The Incarnation, that God took flesh, is the whole reason I am not an Orthodox Jew. The Incarnation is the whole reason I am not lighting a menorah at this time of year. I am a Christian because being a Christian gives me a picture of God to talk to during all these moments where, without the picture, I would forget that God exists. My old professor can't imagine how it can possibly be true that God became man, he can't imagine how I can possibly make sense of it, but I no longer know how to make sense of God, or anything else for that matter, without it.

Here is the thing about God. He is so big and so perfect that we really can't understand Him. We can't possess Him, or apprehend Him. Moses learned this when he climbed up Mount Sinai and saw that the radiance of God's face would burn him up should he gaze upon it directly. But God so wants to be in relationship with us that He makes himself small, smaller than He really is, smaller and more humble than his infinite, perfect self, so that we might be able to get to Him, a little bit.

THINK   "I took all this in and thought it through, inside and out." (Ecclesiastes 9:1)

- "I am a Christian because being a Christian gives me a picture of God to talk to during all these moments where, without the picture, I would forget that God exists." What do you make of Winner's rationale for being a Christian? How close is it to your thinking?
- Winner describes herself as "radically incarnational." What do you think that means? Would you describe yourself that way? Explain.

READ

From *The Magnificent Defeat* by Frederick Buechner[4]

Message in the Stars

We all want to be certain, we all want proof, but the kind of proof that we tend to want—scientifically or philosophically demonstrable proof that would silence all doubts once and for all—would not in the long run, I think, answer the fearful depths of our need at all. For what we need to know, of course, is not just that God exists, not just that beyond the steely brightness of the stars there is a cosmic intelligence of some kind that keeps the whole show going, but that there is a God right here in the thick of our day-by-day lives who may not be writing messages about himself in the stars but who in one way or another is trying to get messages through our blindness as we move around down here knee-deep in the fragrant muck and misery and marvel of the world. It is not objective proof of God's existence that we want but, whether we use religious language for it or not, the experience of God's presence. That is the miracle that we are really after. And that is also, I think, the miracle that we really get.

THINK   "I took all this in and thought it through, inside and out." (Ecclesiastes 9:1)

- If you had to choose between "objective proof of God's existence" and "the experience of God's presence," which do you think you really want in life?
- Describe a recent time when you really experienced God's presence. Was this experience comforting, unsettling, confusing, or what?
- What led you to conclude that this was *God's* presence?

THINK (continued)

PRAY

Slowly read the following poem a couple of times. What speaks to you? Ask God to bring a word or phrase to the surface. Then allow that word or phrase to begin your prayer. It might seem awkward at first. Fine, let it be awkward. But stick with it.

The Dream

Amiably conversant with virtue and evil,
The righteousness of Joseph and wickedness
Of Herod, I'm ever and always a stranger to grace.
I need this annual angel visitation
—Sudden dive by dream to reality—
To know the virgin conceives and God is with us.
The dream powers its way through winter weather
And gives me vision to see the Jesus gift.
Light from the dream lasts a year. Impervious
To equinox and solstice it makes twelve months
Of daylight by which I see the crèche where my
Redeemer lives. Archetypes of praise take shape
Deep in my spirit. As autumn wanes I count
The days 'til I will have the dream again.

—EUGENE PETERSON[5]

LIVE

These words from Peterson serve as a reminder of this section's theme—*incarnation*:

> To know the virgin conceives and God is with us.

You've read from the journal entries, letters, and poems of others. Now it's your turn. What does God want you to live when it comes to *incarnation*? Use the space below to write a letter to yourself. You might want to date the letter so you can reflect later where you were and what was going on in your life regarding *incarnation*.

Date _____

Dear _____

SUFFERING

"There's a lot of suffering to be entered into in this world — the kind of suffering Christ takes on."
(COLOSSIANS 1:24)

Before You Begin

Take just a few moments to still your heart and mind. Remember, God desires to speak to *you* in these moments.

He remembered his Covenant with them,
and, immense with love, took them by the hand.

PSALM 106:45

READ

Colossians 1:24-29

I want you to know how glad I am that it's me sitting here in this jail and not you. There's a lot of suffering to be entered into in this world—the kind of suffering Christ takes on. I welcome the chance to take my share in the church's part of that suffering. When I became a servant in this church, I experienced this suffering as a sheer gift, God's way of helping me serve you, laying out the whole truth.

This mystery has been kept in the dark for a long time, but now it's out in the open. God wanted everyone, not just Jews, to know this rich and glorious secret inside and out, regardless of their background, regardless of their religious standing. The mystery in a nutshell is just this: Christ is in you, so therefore you can look forward to sharing in God's glory. It's that simple. That is the substance of our Message. We preach *Christ*, warning people not to add to the Message. We teach in a spirit of profound common sense so that we can bring each person to maturity. To be mature is to be basic. Christ! No more, no less. That's what I'm working so hard at day after day, year after year, doing my best with the energy God so generously gives me.

THINK   "I took all this in and thought it through, inside and out." (Ecclesiastes 9:1)

- Paul writes, "There's a lot of suffering to be entered into in this world." How does that statement line up with your first view of the Christian life, when you first became a Christian? How about now—has your view changed to accept that suffering will be a part of your faith?
- In this instance, Paul's suffering takes the form of sitting in a jail cell. What form has suffering taken in your life recently?

- In just a few verses, Paul moves from "suffering" to a "rich and glorious secret" to the simplicity of "Christ!" How do you see all of these thoughts connecting in your life? Or are they too far-flung for you to connect? Explain.

READ

From *Lament for a Son* by Nicholas Wolterstorff[1]

(Wolterstorff's son, Eric, was killed in a mountaineering accident at the age of twenty-five.)

God is love. That is why he suffers. To love our suffering sinful world is to suffer. God so suffered for the world that he gave up his only Son to suffering. The one who does not see God's suffering does not see his love. God is suffering love.

So suffering is down at the center of things, deep down where the meaning is. Suffering is the meaning of our world. For Love is the meaning. And Love suffers. The tears of God are the meaning of history.

But mystery remains. Why isn't Love-*with-out*-suffering the meaning of things? Why is *suffering*-Love the meaning? Why does God endure his suffering? Why does he not at once relieve his agony by relieving ours?

THINK

"I took all this in and thought it through, inside and out." (Ecclesiastes 9:1)

- Wolterstorff's phrases seem almost haunting. Write down what emotions each of the following phrases stirs in you:
  "God is suffering love."
  "Suffering is the meaning of our world."
  "The tears of God are the meaning of history."
- Wolterstorff concludes his thoughts with four questions that he calls mysteries. Because they're mysteries, we can't expect to answer them fully. However, you likely have gut feelings as you read those questions. What is your gut telling you?

THINK (continued)

READ

From *For the Time Being* by Annie Dillard[2]

Thinker

(Meister Eckhart, Teilhard de Chardin, Thomas Aquinas, and Baron von Hugel were mystics, theologians, and philosophers in church history.)

Why must we suffer losses? Even Meister Eckhart offers the lame apology that God never intended us to regard his gifts as our property and that "in order to impress it on us, he frequently takes away everything, physical and spiritual. . . . Why does God stress this point so much? Because he wants to be ours exclusively."

It is "fatal," Teilhard said of the old belief that we suffer at the hands of God omnipotent. It is fatal to reason. It does not work. The omnipotence of God makes no sense if it requires the all-causingness of God. Good people quit God altogether at this point . . . perhaps because they last looked into God in their childhoods, and have not changed their views of divinity since. It is not the tooth fairy. In fact, even Aquinas dissolved the fatal problem of natural, physical evil by tinkering with God's omnipotence. As Baron von Hugel noted, Aquinas said that "the Divine Omnipotence must not be taken as the power to effect any imaginable thing, but only the power to effect what is within the nature of things."

Similarly, Teilhard called the explanation that God hides himself deliberately to test our love "hateful"; it is "mental gymnastics." Here: "The doctors of the church explain that the Lord deliberately hides himself from us in order to test our love. One would have to be irretrievably committed to mental gymnastics . . . not to feel the hatefulness of this solution."

THINK   "I took all this in and thought it through, inside and out." (Ecclesiastes 9:1)

- You might have to read this passage several times. What are your general reflections?
- Do you agree or disagree with Eckhart's thought that we suffer because God is testing our love and devotion to him? Have your thoughts about that concept changed as your faith has grown? Explain.
- Teilhard calls Eckhart's notion "hateful." How do you respond to that statement?
- Can you recall a time when you wondered if God was deliberately hiding from you? Did you feel "hated"? If that word is too strong, choose another.

READ

From *Ragman and Other Cries of Faith* by Walter Wangerin Jr.[3]

And Through the Night Watch O'er Your Beds

(Wangerin is the pastor here, walking through the moments before death
with a family. Justine is dying. Her husband is Herman, Bram and Sarah
are her parents, and Irene and Eve are her sisters.)

All Thursday she lay in a coma, with her eyes open.

I declare unto you that when I came to her that evening,
she was beautiful. The irises and pupils were clear, now, though
seeing nothing we could see. The deep brown flesh of her face
had taken every depression of bone; and with her mouth ajar,
as though as the first part of a word, she seemed like nothing so
much as a saint of the early church, aggrieved by a treacherous
pain, yet holy and otherly in her peace.

She was so thin. She was sticks arranged beneath the blan-
kets. I could tell that she was breathing only by the pulsing
underneath her jaw.

Sarah sat in a chair to her left. Something was wrong. The
woman's silence was angry and her lips were pinched.

Bram, too, was silent, now — his back to the wall. . . . He told
me what was wrong. While Sarah was sleeping for a few minutes
in the afternoon, Eve had followed instinct and the request that
she'd heard Justine to make; she invited a manicurist into the
hospital room who was only half-done with Justine's nails when
Sarah returned. Sarah, then, was not pleased by the stranger's
presence at such a personal affair, and tension flashed. . . .

Difficulty. Dear Lord, the air was hard with it. And what was I
to do? . . .

When, past eleven o'clock, I return to her room, Justine lay
center in a little falling light. Right and left of her, each at a distance, were her father and mother, one against the wall and one
in a chair by the curtain. Left and right of her, on the sides of the
bed, holding her hands, were her sisters Irene and Eve — and the
slender fingers of her hands and the deep red of her long nails
were lovely beyond words. . . .

Eve had a linen handkerchief, with which she rubbed the tips of Justine's cuticles, over and over again; and I thought, *What a ministration!* The girl is serving the earthly need of her sister, even now making her beautiful, and how that must feel to Justine and what a comfort to know that this yearning need is being cared for when otherwise she might feel so unlovely! She's holding her hand; but she is also *serving* her in the grasp with a most peculiar love.

THINK   "I took all this in and thought it through, inside and out." (Ecclesiastes 9:1)

• In the Colossians passage, Paul writes, "Christ is in you." How do you see that happening in this reading from Wangerin?

• Have you been ministered to like this before—Christ in a person?

• Have you ministered to someone in this way before? Describe the sense of Christ being in you.

READ

From *The Hungering Dark* by Frederick Buechner[4]

The Sign by the Highway

What is the truth? Take my hand. The truth is not in my hand.
It is not mine to give, is not life's to give. What is the truth? It
is not the answer to any question that we know to ask. Can
there be a truth that saves, can there be a salvation, for those
who have learned of life not to believe in salvation? Only on
the other side of pain, the dream said. On the other side of
the pained embarrassment at the words Jesus saves, which at
its heart is a pained embarrassment at our own nakedness and
incompleteness. . . . On the other side of the pain of the good
thief, which is the pain of surrender, the pain of acknowledging
finally our utter helplessness to save ourselves. In the depths of
his own pain the good thief said, "Jesus, remember me when
you come in your kingly power." Remember me. Remember me.

Jesus said, "I will." He said, preposterously, "Today you will
be with me in Paradise." Spindle-shanked and crackpot, Mary's
boy, God's son, flattened out on the face of a cliff, like a spider
he scrambles up past the four-letter words and the names of
lovers to slap up his preposterous pitch—Jesus saves—and
the preposterousness, the vulgarity almost, of those words
that make us wince is finally, of course, the vulgarity of God
himself. The vulgarity of a God who adorns the sky at sunrise
and sundown with colors no decent painter would dream of
placing together on a single canvas, the vulgarity of a God
who . . . keeps breaking back into the muck of this world. The
vulgarity of a God who was born into a cave among hicks and
the steaming dung of beasts only to grow up and die on a cross
between crooks. The vulgarity of a God who tampers with the
lives of crooks and clowns like me to the point where we come
among crooks and clowns like you with white paint and a brush
of our own and nothing more profound to say, nothing more
precious and crucial to say finally, than just Yes, it is true. He

does save—Jesus. He gives life, he makes whole, and if you choose to be, you will be with him in Paradise.

THINK "I took all this in and thought it through, inside and out." (Ecclesiastes 9:1)

- Choose your favorite sentence or two from this reading. If you could ask Buechner any question about why he wrote those sentences the way he did, what would you ask? Why?
- How do you feel about the use of the word *vulgarity* to describe God? What do you think Buechner is trying to say with that word?
- Buechner writes of Jesus that he "was born into a cave among hicks and the steaming dung of beasts only to grow up and die on a cross between crooks." How do you relate to this ultimate form of humiliation and suffering?

PRAY

Slowly read the following portion of Lamentations a couple of times. What speaks to you? Ask God to bring a word or phrase to the surface. Then allow that word or phrase to begin your prayer. It might seem awkward at first. Fine, let it be awkward. But stick with it.

It's a Good Thing to Hope for Help from God

I'll never forget the trouble, the utter lostness,
    the taste of ashes, the poison I've swallowed.
I remember it all—oh, how well I remember—
    the feeling of hitting the bottom.
But there's one other thing I remember,
    and remembering, I keep a grip on hope:

God's loyal love couldn't have run out,
    his merciful love couldn't have dried up.
They're created new every morning.
    How great your faithfulness!
I'm sticking with God (I say it over and over).
    He's all I've got left.[5]

LIVE

These words from Lamentations serve as a reminder of this section's theme—*suffering*:

>   I'm sticking with GOD (I say it over and over).
>   He's all I've got left.

You've read from the journal entries, letters, and poems of others. Now it's your turn. What does God want you to live when it comes to *suffering*? Use the space below to write a letter to yourself. You might want to date the letter so you can reflect later where you were and what was going on in your life regarding *suffering*.

Date _____

Dear _____

LIVING

"School's out; quit studying the subject and start *living* it!"
(COLOSSIANS 2:7)

Before You Begin

Take just a few moments to still your heart and mind.
Remember, God desires to speak to *you* in these
moments.

> For the sake of the house of our God, GOD,
> I'll do my very best for you.
>
> PSALM 122:9

READ

Colossians 2:2-7

I want you woven into a tapestry of love, in touch with everything there is to know of God. Then you will have minds confident and at rest, focused on Christ, God's great mystery. All the richest treasures of wisdom and knowledge are embedded in that mystery and nowhere else. And we've been shown the mystery! I'm telling you this because I don't want anyone leading you off on some wild-goose chase, after other so-called mysteries, or "the Secret."

VS. 5

I'm a long way off, true, and you may never lay eyes on me, but believe me, I'm on your side, right beside you. I am delighted to hear of the careful and orderly ways you conduct your affairs, and impressed with the solid substance of your faith in Christ.

VS. 6-7

My counsel for you is simple and straightforward: Just go ahead with what you've been given. You received Christ Jesus, the Master; now *live* him. You're deeply rooted in him. You're well constructed upon him. You know your way around the faith. Now do what you've been taught. School's out; quit studying the subject and start *living* it! And let your living spill over into thanksgiving.

THINK   "I took all this in and thought it through, inside and out." (Ecclesiastes 9:1)

- Are there areas in your faith where you don't feel prepared or skilled? Have those areas changed over the years?
- How do you reconcile these feelings with Paul's words that God gave you a mind "confident and at rest, focused on Christ"?
- "Start *living* it!" What do you hear in that phrase? Be specific.

THINK (continued)

READ

From *Action in Waiting* by Christoph Blumhardt[1]

Jesus Needs You, Not Your Religion

Nothing is more dangerous to the advancement of God's kingdom than religion: for it is what makes us heathens. But this is what Christianity has become. Do you not know that it is possible to kill Christ with such Christianity? After all, what is more important—Christianity or Christ? And I'll say even more: we can kill Christ with the Bible! Which is greater: the Bible or Christ? Yes, we can even kill Christ with our prayer. When we approach God with our prayers full of self-love and self-satisfaction, when the aim of our prayers is to make our world great, our prayers are in vain. . . .

The way to serve Jesus, to go to meet God, has not yet been understood. People think they do this with churches, sermons, and worship meetings, but it is not done in this way. This way of doing things has become so rooted in us that it costs a tremendous effort to turn around and find again what will really prepare the way for the kingdom of God.

When Jesus speaks it is always a social matter, a matter for humanity. What Jesus did was to found the cause of God on earth, in order to establish a new society that finally is to include all nations. . . . Faced with this wretched social order, Jesus wants to build a new one. His word to us is this: "You belong to God and not to one of these man-made societies."

THINK   "I took all this in and thought it through, inside and out." (Ecclesiastes 9:1)

- Go back through Paul's words in Colossians 2:2-7 and see if you hear the idea of "religion." If you do, describe it. If you don't, what do you hear instead?

- "When we approach God with our prayers full of self-love and self-satisfaction, when the aim of our prayers is to make our world great, our prayers are in vain." Have you ever been guilty of praying in this way? Why do you think Blumhardt writes that these prayers are in vain?
- What "man-made societies" in your life compete with or even replace your relationship with the living God? What do you think you should do about that?

READ

From *The Sacred Romance* by Brent Curtis and John Eldredge[2]

Less-Wild Lovers

There comes a place on our spiritual journey where renewed religious activity is of no use whatsoever. It is the place where God holds out his hand and asks us to give up our lovers and come and live with him in a much more personal way. It is the place of relational intimacy that Satan lured Adam and Eve away from so long ago in the Garden of Eden. We are both drawn to it and fear it. Part of us would rather return to Scripture memorization, or Bible study, or service—anything that would save us from the unknowns of walking with God. We are partly convinced our life is elsewhere. We are deceived. . . .

The desire God has placed within us is wild in its longing to pursue the One who is unknown. Its capacity and drive is so powerful that it can only be captured momentarily in moments of deep soul communion or sexual ecstasy. And when the moment has passed, we can only hold it as an ache, a haunting of quicksilver that flashes a remembrance of innocence known and lost and, if we have begun to pass into the life of the Beloved, a hope of ecstasies yet to come.

THINK

"I took all this in and thought it through, inside and out." (Ecclesiastes 9:1)

- Has God asked you to give up any "lovers"? How are you doing with that?
- "The desire God has placed within us is wild in its longing to pursue the One who is unknown." What thoughts do you have about this statement? Do you sense this wild desire?

- Do you find yourself occasionally on a "wild-goose chase" (Colossians 2:4), trying to discover some new secret or mystery of the faith? How does that stack up with the idea of pursuing God? Be honest—which chase seems more powerful or attractive to you? Why?

READ

From *Intimate Moments with the Savior* by Ken Gire[3]

An Intimate Moment with Mary and Martha

Finally, she's had enough. Martha throws down the dough and stomps into the living room. "Lord, don't you care that my sister has left me to do the work by myself? Tell her to help me!"

Martha is hot. She doesn't address Mary directly. She's too mad. She doesn't even call her by name. She refers to her as "my sister." And in unsheathing her tongue, she reveals her anger, anger that is double-edged. The one side cuts Jesus, accusing him of lacking concern. The other cuts Mary, accusing her of laziness.

"Martha, Martha." His address is tender and affectionate, yet it has a plaintive tone. . . . "Martha, Martha, you are worried and upset about many things, but only one thing is needed. Mary has chosen what is better, and it will not be taken away from her."

He brings his point gently home: Fellowship with him is a matter of priorities. And a matter of choice. It's the better part of the meal life has to offer. It is, in fact, the main course.

Jesus says something extraordinary about what Mary did: it would become a permanent part of her life; it would count for eternity. Quite a promise.

And what did Mary do? All she did was sit there. It is where she sat that made the difference.

THINK   "I took all this in and thought it through, inside and out." (Ecclesiastes 9:1)

- Read this passage again and reread Colossians 2:2-7 (at the beginning of this Letter). How do you reconcile Mary's "just sitting" with Paul's counsel to "do what you've been taught" and to "start *living*"?
- Where do you most often find yourself—just sitting at Jesus' feet, or living out your faith? Do you think there's need for both? If so, how do you balance the two?

THINK (continued)

READ

From *Abba's Child* by Brennan Manning[4]

The Beloved

(Manning shares an account from Mike Yaconelli, cofounder of Youth Specialties, and his experience of a five-day retreat at the L'Arche community. L'Arche is a community in Toronto, Canada, for mentally and physically handicapped people.)

It only took a few hours of silence before I began to hear my soul speaking. It only took being alone for a short period of time for me to discover I wasn't alone. God had been trying to shout over the noisiness of my life, and I couldn't hear Him. But in the stillness and solitude, his whispers shouted from my soul, "Michael, I am here. I have been calling you, but you haven't been listening. Can you hear me, Michael? I love you. I have always loved you. And I have been waiting for you to hear me say that to you. But you have been so busy trying to prove to yourself you are loved that you have not heard me." . . .

At certain times in all of our lives, we make an adjustment in the course of our lives. This was one of those times for me. If you were to look at a map of my life, you would not be aware of any noticeable difference other than a slight change in direction. I can only tell you that it feels very different now. There is an anticipation, an electricity about God's presence in my life that I have never experienced before. I can only tell you that for the first time in my life I can hear Jesus whisper to me every day, "Michael, I love you. *You are beloved.*" And for some strange reason, that seems to be enough.

THINK   "I took all this in and thought it through, inside and out." (Ecclesiastes 9:1)

- We're all busy; that's a given. The question is, "What are we busy doing?" Ask yourself that question and give your top five answers.

- "You have been so busy trying to prove to yourself you are loved that you have not heard me." Did this make it in your top five? Even if it didn't, go back and see if it's an overall description of your busyness. Maybe it's not, but just check.
- "I love you. I have always loved you." Are those words easy for you to hear from Christ? Explain.

No - I am not always loveable. I don't deserve it.

- School work
- Friendships
- Helping Others / Friends / children
- Bible Study
- House work

PRAY

Slowly read the following poem a couple of times. What speaks to
you? Ask God to bring a word or phrase to the surface. Then allow
that word or phrase to begin your prayer. It might seem awkward at
first. Fine, let it be awkward. But stick with it.

Living

The fire in leaf and grass
so green it seems
each summer the last summer.

The wind blowing, the leaves
shivering in the sun,
each day the last day.

A red salamander
so cold and so
easy to catch, dreamily

moves his delicate feet
and long tail. I hold
my hand open for him to go.

Each minute the last minute.

—DENISE LEVERTOV[5]

- Living as if it is your last day.

*- oy living to the utmost as if
it could never happen again.*

LIVE

These words from Levertov serve as a reminder of this section's theme—*living*:

Each minute the last minute.

You've read from the journal entries, letters, and poems of others. Now it's your turn. What does God want you to live when it comes to *living*? Use the space below to write a letter to yourself. You might want to date the letter so you can reflect later where you were and what was going on in your life regarding *living*.

Date _____

Dear *Father* _____ :

Help me to Prioritize & and be still and know that you are God. Help me to know I am loved so I can love others

"God brought you alive — right along with Christ!"
(COLOSSIANS 2:14)

Before You Begin

Take just a few moments to still your heart and mind.
Remember, God desires to speak to *you* in these
moments.

> *I'll stride freely through wide open spaces*
> *as I look for your truth and your wisdom.*
>
> PSALM 119:46

READ

Colossians 2:8-15

Watch out for people who try to dazzle you with big words and intellectual double-talk. They want to drag you off into endless arguments that never amount to anything. They spread their ideas through the empty traditions of human beings and the empty superstitions of spirit beings. But that's not the way of Christ. Everything of God gets expressed in him, so you can see and hear him clearly. You don't need a telescope, a microscope, or a horoscope to realize the fullness of Christ, and the emptiness of the universe without him. When you come to him, that fullness comes together for you, too. His power extends over everything.

Entering into this fullness is not something you figure out or achieve. It's not a matter of being circumcised or keeping a long list of laws. No, you're already *in*—insiders—not through some secretive initiation rite but rather through what Christ has already gone through for you, destroying the power of sin. If it's an initiation ritual you're after, you've already been through it by submitting to baptism. Going under the water was a burial of your old life; coming up out of it was a resurrection, God raising you from the dead as he did Christ. When you were stuck in your old sin-dead life, you were incapable of responding to God. God brought you alive—right along with Christ! Think of it! All sins forgiven, the slate wiped clean, that old arrest warrant canceled and nailed to Christ's cross. He stripped all the spiritual tyrants in the universe of their sham authority at the Cross and marched them naked through the streets.

THINK   "I took all this in and thought it through, inside and out." (Ecclesiastes 9:1)

- Do you ever still feel stuck in a "sin-dead life"? What concerns you most about that?

- "Entering into this fullness [of Christ] is not something you figure out or achieve." What do you think Paul means with this sentence? In what parts of your faith do you wrestle with trying to "figure out or achieve"? Explain.

READ

From *The River Why* by David James Duncan[1]

Concerning Statistics

Like gamblers, baseball fans and television networks, fishermen are enamored of statistics. The adoration of statistics is a trait so deeply embedded in their nature that even those rarefied anglers the disciples of Jesus couldn't resist backing their yarns with arithmetic: when the resurrected Christ appears on the morning shore of the Sea of Galilee and directs his forlorn and skunked disciples to the famous catch of *John 21*, we learn that the net contained not "a boatload" of fish, nor "about a hundred and a half," nor "over a gross," but precisely "an hundred and fifty and three." This is, it seems to me, one of the most remarkable statistics ever computed. Consider the circumstances: this is *after* the Crucifixion and the Resurrection; Jesus is standing on the beach newly risen from the dead, and it is only the third time the disciples have seen him since the nightmare of Calvary. And yet we learn that in the net there were "great fishes" numbering precisely "an hundred and fifty and three." How was this digit discovered? Mustn't it have happened thus: upon hauling the net to shore, the disciples squatted down by that immense, writhing fish pile and started tossing them into a second pile, painstakingly counting "one, two, three, four, five, six, seven . . ." all the way up to an hundred and fifty and three, while the newly risen Lord of Creation, the Sustainer of their beings, He who died for them and for Whom they would gladly die, stood waiting, ignored, till the heap of fish was quantified. Such is the fisherman's compulsion toward rudimentary mathematics!

THINK   "I took all this in and thought it through, inside and out." (Ecclesiastes 9:1)

- What's your reaction to Duncan's words? How does it make Jesus' disciples seem more real to you?

- For the disciples, the issue was counting fish. But what about your life? What tends to dazzle you to the extent that if the newly risen Lord were standing right there, he'd have to wait until you were finished? No points for being super-spiritual here. What consumes you that, after the fact, really doesn't amount to anything?

- Do you have an awareness of when you're being drawn in to the "dazzle," or do you usually realize it only in hindsight?

READ

From *Lake Wobegon Days* by Garrison Keillor[2]

Protestant

Our Lake Wobegon bunch was part of a Sanctified Brethren branch known as the Cox Brethren, which was one of a number of "exclusive" Brethren branches—that is, to *non*-Coxians, we were known as "Cox Brethren"; to ourselves, we were simply *The* Brethren, the last remnant of the true Church. Our name came from Brother Cox in South Dakota who was kicked out of the Johnson Brethren in 1932—for preaching the truth! So naturally my Grandpa and most of our family went with Mr. Cox and formed the new fellowship.

The split with the Johnsons was triggered by Mr. Johnson's belief that what was abominable to God in the Old Testament must be abominable still, which he put forward at the Grace & Truth Bible Conference in Rapid City in 1932. Mr. Cox stood up and walked out, followed by others. The abomination doctrine not only went against the New Covenant of Grace principle, it opened up rich new areas of controversy in the vast annals of Jewish law. Should Brethren then refrain from pork, meat that God had labeled "Unclean"? Were we to be thrown into the maze of commandments laid out in Leviticus and Deuteronomy, where we are told to smite our enemies with the sword and stone to death rebellious children?

Mr. Johnson's sermon was against women's slacks, and he had quoted Deuteronomy 22:5, "The woman shall not wear that which pertaineth unto a man, neither shall a man put on a woman's garment: for all that do so are abomination unto the Lord thy God," but Mr. Cox, though he was hardly pro-slacks, felt Mr. Johnson failed to emphasize grace as having superseded the law, and when Mr. Johnson said, "An abomination to God under the law is still an abomination to God under grace," Mr. Cox smelled the burning rubber of Error and stood up and marched. He and the other walkouts proceeded to a grove of trees and prayed for Mr.

Johnson's soul, and Mr. Johnson and those seated inside did the same for them. The split was never repaired, though as a result of being thought in favor of slacks, the Cox Brethren became death on the subject. My mother never wore slacks, though she did dress my sister in winter leggings, which troubled Grandpa. "It's not the leggings so much as what they represent and what they could lead to," he told her. He thought that baby boys should not wear sleepers unless they were the kind with snaps up the legs. Mother pointed out that the infant Jesus was wrapped in swaddling clothes. "That doesn't mean he wore a dress," Grandpa said. "They probably wrapped his legs separately."

THINK   "I took all this in and thought it through, inside and out." (Ecclesiastes 9:1)

- Did Keillor's words make you chuckle? Why or why not?
- If you take a walk down your own "religious" memory lane, do you find moments of division like these on the path? Tell that story as best you can. How does the story end? How long ago did it happen?
- Keillor's church split "was never repaired." In your story, did the experience harm or shake your faith? Have you ever asked God to help repair the damage? Explain.

READ

From *Waking the Dead* by John Eldredge[3]

Walking with God

When we set out to hear God's voice, we do not listen as though it will come from somewhere above us or in the room around us. It comes to us from *within*, in the heart, the dwelling place of God. Now, most of us haven't been trained in this, and it's going to take a little practice "tuning in" to all that's going on in there. And there's a lot going on in there, by the way. Many things are trying to play upon the beautiful instrument of the heart. Advertisers are constantly trying to pull on your heartstrings. So is your boss. The devil is a master at manipulating the heart. So are many people—though they would never admit that is what they are doing. How will you know what is compelling you? "Who can map out the various forces at play in one soul?" asked Augustine, a man who was the first to write out the story of listening to his heart. "Man is a great depth, O Lord . . . but the hairs of his head are easier by far to count than . . . the movements of his heart."

This can be distressing at times. All sorts of awful things can seem to issue from your heart—anger, lust, fear, petty jealousies. If you think it's you, a reflection of what's really going on in your heart, it will disable you. It could stop your journey dead in its tracks.

THINK "I took all this in and thought it through, inside and out." (Ecclesiastes 9:1)

- Reread Paul's words from Colossians 2:8-15 at the beginning of this Letter. How does it match up with what Eldredge writes here?

- Most of us battle both external clatter and inner voices as we try to discern what God is saying to us. How do you sort out all the noise? Make sure to talk about this with your group—you might be able to help each other hear God more clearly.

READ

From *Between Noon and Three* by Robert Farrar Capon[4]

Spirituality vs. Grace

There is no way of tying the kingdom of heaven to anything we do. It comes because the King makes it come, not because we give it a helping hand. . . .

The Reformers, you see, were dead right on this subject. . . . Read Luther sometime on the subject of clerical celibacy. The Reformation was a time when people went blind-staggering drunk because they had discovered, in the dusty basement of late medievalism, a whole cellarful of fifteen-hundred-year-old, 200-proof grace—of bottle after bottle of pure distillate of Scripture that would convince anyone that God saves us single-handed. The Word of the Gospel . . . suddenly turned out to be a flat announcement that the saved were home free even before they started. How foolish, then, they said, how reprehensibly mislead-ing, they said, to take the ministers of that Word of free, unquali-fied acceptance and slap enforced celibacy on them—to make their lives bear a sticker that said they had gone an extra mile and paid an extra toll. It was simply to hide the light of grace under a bushel of pseudo-law, to take the sacrament of the Mystery and go out of the way to make it look as little like the Mystery as pos-sible. And for the Reformers, that was a crime. Grace was to be drunk neat: no water, no ice, and certainly no ginger ale; neither goodness, nor badness, nor the flowers that bloom in the spring of super-spirituality could be allowed to enter into the case.

THINK   "I took all this in and thought it through, inside and out." (Ecclesiastes 9:1)

- Do you ever find yourself trying to earn points with God in your relationship with him? Why do you think Christians fall into that trap so easily?

- ". . . to make their lives bear a sticker that said they had gone an extra mile and paid an extra toll." Do you ever sense that your faith requires this of you? Explain.
- "Grace was to be drunk neat: no water, no ice, and certainly no ginger ale." Recall a time when you experienced God's pure grace. Share that story in as much detail as you can.

PRAY

Slowly read the following poem a couple of times. What speaks to you? Ask God to bring a word or phrase to the surface. Then allow that word or phrase to begin your prayer. It might seem awkward at first. Fine, let it be awkward. But stick with it.

I Don't Pray So Very Well

I don't pray so very well
  With all the levels of divine contact newly devised
And all the assorted certainties of those who know
  Far more about God than perhaps He does Himself.
I'm still in the back pew with the publican,
Struggling to believe, pushing through today's pain,
  And worried about what's in store for tomorrow.
I hand on to simple things like a Father Who never
  Gives a stone when I ask Him for bread.
Some of the greatest gifts I received were when
  I never asked at all.
When a loving, unseen hand took me safely along
  Some precipices I'd not like to walk again.
God is still a mystery to me and my faith is probably
  As weak as any man's alive.
But I never quit believing in love and joy and serenity,
And knowing that somehow I am a favored son
  Whether I deserve it or not.
Our relationship keeps getting simpler:
  I picture the kind of man I really want to be,
And in bits and pieces He gives me the help to be it.

—JAMES KAVANAUGH[5]

LIVE

These words from Kavanaugh serve as a reminder of this section's
theme—*grace*:

> And knowing that somehow I am a favored son
> Whether I deserve it or not.

You've read from the journal entries, letters, and poems of
others. Now it's your turn. What does God want you to live when it
comes to *grace*? Use the space below to write a letter to yourself. You
might want to date the letter so you can reflect later where you were
and what was going on in your life regarding *grace*.

Date _____

Dear _____

CHOICE

"Don't tolerate people who try to run your life."
(COLOSSIANS 2:18)

Before You Begin

Take just a few moments to still your heart and mind. Remember, God desires to speak to *you* in these moments.

I reject made-in-Canaan gods,
stay clear of contamination.

PSALM 101:3

READ

Colossians 2:16-23

So don't put up with anyone pressuring you in details of diet, worship services, or holy days. All those things are mere shadows cast before what was to come; the substance is Christ.

Don't tolerate people who try to run your life, ordering you to bow and scrape, insisting that you join their obsession with angels and that you seek out visions. They're a lot of hot air, that's all they are. They're completely out of touch with the source of life, Christ, who puts us together in one piece, whose very breath and blood flow through us. He is the Head and we are the body. We can grow up healthy in God only as he nourishes us.

So, then, if with Christ you've put all that pretentious and infantile religion behind you, why do you let yourselves be bullied by it? "Don't touch this! Don't taste that! Don't go near this!" Do you think things that are here today and gone tomorrow are worth that kind of attention? Such things sound impressive if said in a deep enough voice. They even give the illusion of being pious and humble and ascetic. But they're just another way of showing off, making yourselves look important.

THINK   "I took all this in and thought it through, inside and out." (Ecclesiastes 9:1)

- Do you have people who try to "run your life"? How do they do that? Do you have any clue why they try to run your life?
- Answer the same questions with your faith in mind: Do you have people who try to "run your life" of faith? How do they do that? Do you have any clue why they try to run your faith life?
- React to this phrase: "showing off, making yourselves look important." Who comes to mind when you think of this phrase? Have you ever been guilty of doing this? Explain.

THINK (continued)

READ

From *The Jesus I Never Knew* by Philip Yancey[1]

Mission

Jews in Jesus' day envisioned a ladder reaching higher and higher towards God, a hierarchy expressed in the very architecture of the temple. Gentiles and "half-breeds" like the Samaritans were permitted only in the outer Court of the Gentiles; a wall separated them from the next partition, which admitted Jewish women. Jewish men could proceed one stage further, but only priests could enter the sacred areas. Finally, only one priest, the high priest, could enter the Most Holy Place, and that just once a year on the day of Yom Kippur.

The society was, in effect, a religious caste system based on steps toward holiness, and the Pharisees' scrupulosity reinforced the system daily. All their rules on washing hands and avoiding defilement were an attempt to make themselves acceptable to God. Had not God set forth lists of desirable (spotless) and undesirable (flawed, unclean) animals for use in sacrifice? Had not God banned sinners, menstruating women, the physically deformed, and other "undesirables" from the temple? The Qumram community of the Essenes made a firm rule, "No madman, or lunatic, or simpleton, or fool, no blind man, or maimed, or lame, or deaf man, and no minor, shall enter into the Community."

In the midst of this religious caste system, Jesus appeared. To the Pharisees' dismay he had no qualms about socializing with children or sinners or even Samaritans. He touched, or was touched by, the "unclean": those with leprosy, the deformed, a hemorrhaging woman, the lunatic and possessed. Although Levitical laws prescribed a day of purification after touching a sick person, Jesus conducted mass healings in which he touched scores of sick people; he never concerned himself with the rules of defilement after contact with the sick or even the dead.

THINK   "I took all this in and thought it through, inside and out." (Ecclesiastes 9:1)

- Consider your faith journey from its start until now. What would you list as five steps toward holiness that you've been taught, heard from pastors, read in books, and so forth? There might be more than five, but let's start there.

- Could you consider those steps as a type of "religious caste system"? Why or why not?

- Paul writes, "They're completely out of touch with the source of life, Christ." Yancey writes, "In the midst of this religious caste system, Jesus appeared." In your own words, flesh out what Paul and Yancey are getting at. You don't have to compose a polished essay—just list some thoughts that help you make sense of what they're saying.

READ

From *Walking on Water* by Madeleine L'Engle[2]

Keeping the Clock Wound

Freedom is a terrible gift, and the theory behind all dictatorships is that "the people" do not want freedom. They want bread and circuses. They want workman's compensation and fringe benefits and TV. Give up your free will, give up your freedom to make choices, listen to the expert, and you will have three cars in your garage, steak on the table, and you will no longer have to suffer the agony of choice. . . .

A series of mistaken choices throughout the centuries has brought us to a restricted way of life in which we have less freedom than we are meant to have, and so we have a sense of powerlessness and frustration which comes from our inability to change the many terrible things happening on our planet.

All the Faust stories are studies in the results of choice. Dostoyevsky's story of the Grand Inquisitor in *The Brothers Karamazov* is one of the most brilliant pieces of Christian writing that I know, and one of the most frightening, because the Grand Inquisitor, like many dictators, is plausible; he wants people to be happy; he does not want them to suffer; the Church, because of the great love it has for humanity, has done its best to reverse all the damage caused by Jesus, with his terrible promise of the truth that will make us free. We do not want to be free, the Grand Inquisitor assures Jesus. We want these stones to be turned into bread.

THINK   "I took all this in and thought it through, inside and out." (Ecclesiastes 9:1)

- L'Engle's main point: People don't really want freedom. Do you agree with her? Why or why not?
- Give your reaction to these phrases:
  "freedom is a terrible gift"

"listen to the expert"

"the agony of choice"

"the damage caused by Jesus, with his terrible promise of
the truth"

- So what do you hear in this passage? A rebel-with-a-cause
commercial? Don't let "the man" bring you down? Tell the
establishment they can shove it? Reread Colossians 2:16-
23 at the beginning of this Letter. How closely do L'Engle's
thoughts match up with Paul's?

READ

From *Charlotte's Web* by E. B. White[3]

Wilbur's Escape

"Ho-*mer*!" she cried. "Pig's out! Lurvy! Pig's out! Homer! Lurvy! Pig's out. He's down there under that apple tree."

"Now the trouble starts," thought Wilbur. "Now I'll catch it."

The goose heard the racket and she, too, started hollering. "Run-run-run downhill, make for the woods, the woods!" she shouted to Wilbur. "They'll never-never-never catch you in the woods."

The cocker spaniel heard the commotion, and he ran out from the barn to join in the chase. Mr. Zuckerman heard, and he came out of the machine shed where he was mending a tool. Lurvy, the hired man, heard the noise and came up from the asparagus patch where he was pulling weeds. Everybody walked toward Wilbur, and Wilbur didn't know what to do. The woods seemed a long way off, and anyway, he had never been down there in the woods and wasn't sure he would like it.

"Get around behind him Lurvy," said Mr. Zuckerman, "and drive him toward the barn! And take it easy—don't rush him! I'll go and get a bucket of slops."

The news of Wilbur's escape spread rapidly among the animals on the place. Whenever any creature broke loose on Zuckerman's farm, the event was of great interest to the others. The goose shouted to the nearest cow that Wilbur was free, and soon all the cows knew. Then one of the cows told one of the sheep, and soon all the sheep knew. The lambs learned about it from their mothers. The horses, in their stalls in the barn, pricked up their ears when they heard the goose hollering; and soon the horses had caught on to what was happening. "Wilbur's out," they said. Every animal stirred its head and became excited to know that one of its friends had got free and was no longer penned up or tied fast.

Wilbur didn't know what to do or which way to run. It

seemed as though everybody was after him. "If this is what it's like to be free," he thought, "I believe I'd rather be penned up in my own yard."

THINK   "I took all this in and thought it through, inside and out." (Ecclesiastes 9:1)

- Go back through White's wonderful story and mark what spoke to you. Talk about those words or phrases with your group; why did you highlight them?
- Wilbur said, "If this is what it's like to be free . . . I believe I'd rather be penned up in my own yard." When it comes to a life of faith, which do you think is the right choice—making a break for the freedom of the woods, or returning to the safety of the pen? Is this right choice always the same, or different at different times?

READ

From *Jonathan Livingston Seagull: A Story* by Richard Bach[4]

Centered for Shame

(Jonathan Seagull has stood in opposition to the dignity and tradition of
the Gull Family: Gulls are put into this world to eat and stay alive as long
as possible. Jonathan has discovered new realms of flight and freedom
that have gained him the title "outcast" from his fellow gulls.)

Jonathan Seagull spent the rest of his days alone, but he flew out beyond the Far Cliffs. His one sorrow was not solitude, it was that the other gulls refused to believe the glory of flight that awaited them; they refused to open their eyes and see.

He learned more each day. He learned that a stream-lined high-speed dive could bring him to find the rare and tasty fish that schooled ten feet below the surface of the ocean: he no longer needed fishing boats and stale bread for survival. He learned to sleep in the air, setting a course at night across the offshore wind, covering a hundred miles from sunset to sunrise. With the same inner control, he flew through heavy sea-fogs and climbed above them into dazzling clear skies . . . in the very times when every other gull stood on the ground, knowing nothing but mist and rain. He learned to ride the high winds far inland, to dine there on delicate insects.

What he had once hoped for the Flock, he now gained for himself alone; he learned to fly, and was not sorry for the price that he had paid. Jonathan Seagull discovered that boredom and fear and anger are the reasons that a gull's life is so short, and with these gone from his thought, he lived a long fine life indeed.

THINK   "I took all this in and thought it through, inside and out." (Ecclesiastes 9:1)

- How prevalent are "boredom and fear and anger" in your life? If you separated your spiritual life from everything else, would your answer change? Be honest.

- With all the emphasis these days on "community," what's your response to the "solitary" aspect of Jonathan's story? Are community and solitude in tension with one another? Or do they complement each other somehow? Explain.
- "His one sorrow was not solitude, it was that the other gulls refused to believe the glory of flight that awaited them; they refused to open their eyes and see." Have you felt this kind of sorrow before? When and where and what? Think a little.

PRAY

Slowly read the following poem a couple of times. What speaks to you? Ask God to bring a word or phrase to the surface. Then allow that word or phrase to begin your prayer. It might seem awkward at first. Fine, let it be awkward. But stick with it.

Just As the Calendar Began to Say Summer

I went out of the schoolhouse fast
and through the gardens and to the woods,
and spent all summer forgetting what I'd been taught—

two times two, and diligence, and so forth,
how to be modest and useful, and how to succeed and so forth,
machines and oil and plastic and money and so forth.

By fall I had healed somewhat, but was summoned back
to the chalky rooms and the desks, to sit and remember

the way the river kept rolling its pebbles,
the way the wild wrens sang though they hadn't a penny in the
    bank,
the way the flowers were dressed in nothing but light.

—MARY OLIVER[5]

LIVE

These words from Oliver serve as a reminder of this section's theme—*choice*:

> I went out of the schoolhouse . . .
> and spent all summer forgetting what I'd been taught.

You've read from the journal entries, letters, and poems of others. Now it's your turn. What does God want you to live when it comes to *choice*? Use the space below to write a letter to yourself. You might want to date the letter so you can reflect later where you were and what was going on in your life regarding *choice*.

Date _____

Dear _____

REAL LIFE

"Your old life is dead."
(Colossians 3:3)

Before You Begin

Take just a few moments to still your heart and mind. Remember, God desires to speak to *you* in these moments.

My question: What are God-worshipers like?
Your answer: Arrows aimed at God's bull's-eye.
PSALM 25:12

READ

Colossians 3:1-8

So if you're serious about living this new resurrection life with Christ, *act* like it. Pursue the things over which Christ presides. Don't shuffle along, eyes to the ground, absorbed with the things right in front of you. Look up, and be alert to what is going on around Christ—that's where the action is. See things from *his* perspective.

Your old life is dead. Your new life, which is your *real* life—even though invisible to spectators—is with Christ in God. *He* is your life. When Christ (your real life, remember) shows up again on this earth, you'll show up, too—the real you, the glorious you. Meanwhile, be content with obscurity, like Christ.

And that means killing off everything connected with that way of death: sexual promiscuity, impurity, lust, doing whatever you feel like whenever you feel like it, and grabbing whatever attracts your fancy. That's a life shaped by things and feelings instead of by God. It's because of this kind of thing that God is about to explode in anger. It wasn't long ago that you were doing all that stuff and not knowing any better. But you know better now, so make sure it's all gone for good: bad temper, irritability, meanness, profanity, dirty talk.

THINK   "I took all this in and thought it through, inside and out." (Ecclesiastes 9:1)

- Paul writes, "Be content with obscurity, like Christ." What do you think he means? Talk this one over with your group.
- Think through the last three months of your life. What attracted your fancy? What "things and feelings" have you allowed to consume your thoughts, time, attention, money?

- "Your new life, which is your *real* life—even though invisible to spectators—is with Christ in God." Why do you think Paul calls the real life "invisible"? Does he mean something to be hidden away, a life that isn't distinguished, impossible for unbelievers to understand, or what? Explain.

READ

From *Ordinarily Sacred* by Lynda Sexson[1]

Introductory Note

There are no inherently sacred objects, events, or thoughts; they are made sacred by a special context. The usual, recognizable context of the sacred is an institutional or traditional setting through which the culture agrees that something has sacred content. What about those special—or metaphorically saturated—contents that burst out of traditional confines, or never find their way into them? If there is no political body to verify occurrences or images as religious or sacred, would these particularized events or images still have special connotations? Might we call that "sacred" or this "religious"? Without referring to those overwhelming, transforming experiences that occur somewhat rarely in human life, there are universal experiences which are common yet set apart, ordinary yet consummately extraordinary, mundane yet sacred. . . .

The sacred, when not bound up by politics or economics, is nearer to something we call the aesthetic. Both the religious and the aesthetic are informed by and produce an effect on the worldviews from which they arise. In some sense then, art and religion can be described as the notation of moments which discover or rediscover one's worldview, create or re-create one's philosophical depth. Art is the creation of an imaginative universe. Religion is the creation of an imaginative . . . universe—and the entering into the creation. . . .

The sacred quality of our lives is fabricated from the metaphors we make. We can discover or recognize the sacred within the secular, or the divine in the ordinary.

THINK   "I took all this in and thought it through, inside and out." (Ecclesiastes 9:1)

- You might have to reread Sexson's words; she's touching on deep things here. What are your initial reactions to this passage? Anything you really like? Dislike? Are totally lost on?
- Sexson advocates a view that the ordinary—those things right in front of us—might contain the sacred. Can you think of experiences in your life where that has been true? However, Paul says not to become "absorbed with the things right in front of you." Are these opposing thoughts? Explain.

READ

From *The Alphabet of Grace* by Frederick Buechner[2]

Sibilants

You are the world's to name. And yet not. The world is yours to name. It is your birthday, and it is you who must give yourself birth, put back together a self again out of all these rags and bobtails. Night has wiped the slate, if not clean as a hound's tooth, at least clean enough. Follow where your feet take you.

You do not so much have a body as you are a body with slapstick needs that must be attended to before you can attend very effectively to anything else. . . . With razor in hand and soap on your chin, you read among other things your doom in your face, the failures, estrangements, betrayals and self-betrayals. And you read mortality in your face—this is the face that you will die with, the face that you will die of. But you read also hope in your face—the hope that by the grace of this new day you may become somehow better than your face. You wash. Because you belong to a race of creatures who hide their nakedness from another, you dress—the lunacy of all those tubes of cloth for arms and legs, those buttons, buckles and flaps. But you are no hero; you dress. And washed, dressed, part hidden, part forgiven, part awake, part named . . . the question is, What's to be done? What's to be done.

THINK

"I took all this in and thought it through, inside and out." (Ecclesiastes 9:1)

- Write down your daily regimen, from the moment you wake up to the moment you climb back into bed. Some days are different, but what's the common or usual? How do you reconcile your day with Paul's encouragement, "Don't shuffle along, eyes to the ground, absorbed with the things right in front of you"?

- "You read among other things your doom in your face, the failures, estrangements, betrayals and self-betrayals. . . . But you read also hope in your face." Do you know what Buechner's talking about? Have you ever looked into the mirror and seen either doom or hope? Elaborate.

READ

From *The Awakened Heart* by Gerald May[3]

The Life of the Heart

In one way or another, we all know what it is to relinquish our freedom for love.

It is critical to understand what freedom means here. Because love is a giving of ourselves, it always involves some choice to direct and restrain our behavior. Love means being willing to make sacrifices for someone or something. When we love, we do not follow every impulse that comes along. We have a higher concern, a deeper desire; we value our beloved more than we value our passing whims. The freedom question, then, is not whether we can do whatever we want but whether we can do what we *most deeply* want.

It is a critical distinction; please take care to understand it. The difference is between attachment-binding desire and commitment-honoring desire. It is the difference between codependence and compassion, between neediness and mutuality, between shame and dignity.

Only we ourselves are responsible when we sell out our freedom: when we put up with abuse, when we abuse ourselves with substances, when we do destructive things in order to maintain our jobs, relationships, possessions, or self-images. Yet it is not a simple matter of willpower or strength of character. We are responsible for our addictive behavior, but we feel powerless to control it. If anything is hell for the human will, this is.

THINK "I took all this in and thought it through, inside and out." (Ecclesiastes 9:1)

- Do any of May's words ring true for you? If not, that's fine. But if so, what applies to your life?
- In Colossians 3:5, Paul urges against "doing whatever you feel like whenever you feel like it." Here, May writes, "When

we love, we do not follow every impulse that comes along."
How would you put this aspect of the Christian life into your
own words?

- How do you distinguish between doing whatever you want
and doing whatever you *most deeply* want?

READ

From *A River Runs Through It* by Norman Maclean[4]

Shadow Casting

(The narrator is Norman Maclean. His brother, Paul, is demonstrating the art of "shadow casting." The Big Blackfoot is a river in Montana, and "Rainbow" refers to Rainbow trout.)

The river above and below his rock was all big Rainbow water, and he would cast hard and low upstream, skimming the water with his fly but never letting it touch. Then he would pivot, reverse his line in a great oval above his head, and drive his line low and hard downstream, again skimming the water with his fly. He would complete this grand circle four or five times, creating an immensity of motion which culminated in nothing if you did not know, even if you could not see, that now somewhere out there a small fly was washing itself on a wave. Shockingly, immensity would return as the Big Blackfoot and the air above it became iridescent with the arched sides of a great Rainbow.

He called this "shadow casting," and frankly I don't know whether to believe the theory behind it—that the fish are alerted by the shadows of flies passing over the water by the first casts, so hit the fly the moment it touches the water. . . .

I heard voices behind me, and a man and his wife came down the trail, each carrying a rod, but probably they weren't going to do much fishing. Probably they intended nothing much more than to enjoy being out of doors with each other and, on the side, to pick enough huckleberries for a pie. In those days there was little in the way of rugged sports clothes for women, and she was a big, rugged woman and wore regular men's bib overalls, and her motherly breasts bulged out of the bib. She was the first to see my brother pivoting on the top of his cliff. To her, he must have looked something like a trick rope artist at a rodeo, doing everything except jumping in and out of his loops.

She kept watching while groping behind her to smooth out some pine needles to sit on. "My, my!" she said.

Her husband stopped and stood and said, "Jesus." Every now

and then he said, "Jesus." Each time his wife nodded. She was one of America's mothers who never dream of using profanity themselves but enjoy their husbands', and later come to need it, like cigar smoke.

THINK   "I took all this in and thought it through, inside and out." (Ecclesiastes 9:1)

- The apostle Paul said to make sure that all "profanity" and "dirty talk" were "gone for good." Do you think this is an example of what he's talking about?
- Debate this in your group. Whether you said "yes" or "no," defend your answer.

PRAY

Slowly read the following poem a couple of times. What speaks to you? Ask God to bring a word or phrase to the surface. Then allow that word or phrase to begin your prayer. It might seem awkward at first. Fine, let it be awkward. But stick with it.

Dilemma

I want to be
　　famous
so I can be
　　humble
about being
　　famous.

What good is my
　　humility
when I am
　　stuck
in this
　　obscurity?

— DAVID BUDBILL[5]

LIVE

These words from Budbill serve as a reminder of this section's
theme—*real life*:

> What good is my humility
> when I am stuck in this obscurity?

You've read from the journal entries, letters, and poems of
others. Now it's your turn. What does God want you to live when it
comes to *real life*? Use the space below to write a letter to yourself.
You might want to date the letter so you can reflect later where you
were and what was going on in your life regarding *real life*.

Date _____

Dear _____

"Don't lie to one another. You're done with that old
life. . . . From now on everyone is defined by Christ."
(COLOSSIANS 3:9,11)

Before You Begin

Take just a few moments to still your heart and mind.
Remember, God desires to speak to *you* in these
moments.

> *I hate lies—can't stand them!*
>
> PSALM 119:163

READ

Colossians 3:9-11

Don't lie to one another. You're done with that old life. It's like a filthy set of ill-fitting clothes you've stripped off and put in the fire. Now you're dressed in a new wardrobe. Every item of your new way of life is custom-made by the Creator, with his label on it. All the old fashions are now obsolete. Words like Jewish and non-Jewish, religious and irreligious, insider and outsider, uncivilized and uncouth, slave and free, mean nothing. From now on everyone is defined by Christ, everyone is included in Christ.

THINK
"I took all this in and thought it through, inside and out." (Ecclesiastes 9:1)

- What was the last lie you told? Did anyone find out about it? Did you fess up?
- Paul writes, "From now on everyone is defined by Christ, everyone is included in Christ." How do you think that relates to lying? There might not be one "right" answer here—just your own reflections. Reread the passage if you get stuck.

READ

From *People of the Lie* by M. Scott Peck[1]

The Father of Lies

(Peck's words come via several experiences in actual exorcisms.
Peck refers to Satan as an "it.")

In fact, *the only power that Satan has is through human belief in its lies.* . . .

So we are back to lies. Whatever relationship it might have to the "people of the lie," I know no more accurate epithet for Satan than the Father of Lies. Throughout both exorcisms it lied continually. Even when it revealed itself, it did so with half-truths. It was revealed to be the Antichrist when it said, "We don't hate Jesus, we just test him." But the reality is that it does hate Jesus.

The list of lies it spoke was endless—sometimes almost a boring litany. The major ones I remember were: humans must defend themselves in order to survive and cannot rely on anything other than themselves in their defense; everything is explainable in terms of negative and positive energy . . . and there is no mystery in the world; love is a thought and has no objective reality; science is whatever one chooses to call science; death is the absolute end to life—there is no more; all humans are motivated primarily by money, and if this appears not to be the case, it is only because they are hypocrites; to compete for money, therefore, is the only intelligent way to live.

Satan can use any human sin or weakness. . . . But its principal weapon is fear.

THINK

"I took all this in and thought it through, inside and out." (Ecclesiastes 9:1)

- Peck asserts his belief that "the Father of Lies" is the most accurate name for Satan. Do you agree or disagree?
- What about the following lies that Satan claimed? Do you agree or disagree with these? Be sure to explain your answer.

"Humans must defend themselves in order to survive."
"There is no mystery in the world."
"Love is a thought and has no objective reality."

- Are you dedicated to reality at all costs? What makes you think so?

READ

From *Wild at Heart* by John Eldredge[2]

A Battle to Fight

(When Eldredge refers to something that happened in "traffic," he means
a fight that he and his wife had, a fight that had no grounds in reality.)

The devil no doubt has a place in our theology, but is he a category we even think about in the daily events of our lives? Has it ever crossed your mind that not every thought that crosses your mind comes from you? What I experienced in the midst of traffic . . . happens all the time in marriages, in ministries, in any relationship. We are being lied to all the time. Yet we never stop to say, "Wait a minute . . . who else is speaking here? Where are those ideas coming from? Where are those feelings coming from?" If you read the saints from every age before the Modern Era—the pride-filled age of reason, science and technology we all were thoroughly educated in—you'll find that they take the devil very seriously indeed. As Paul says, "We are not unaware of his schemes" (2 Cor. 2:11). But we, the enlightened, have a much more commonsense approach to things. We look for a psychological or physical or even political explanation for every trouble we meet.

THINK
"I took all this in and thought it through, inside and out." (Ecclesiastes 9:1)

- Have you ever considered that your thoughts might not be your own thoughts? Why or why not? What would it mean if someone were always lying to you?
- Do you take the Devil seriously? Was that mindset a part of your training in the early days of your faith? Explain.
- Eldredge writes, "We look for a psychological or physical or even political explanation for every trouble we meet." Do you ever find it difficult to attribute your troubles to

the work of Satan? Why do you think our modern culture struggles with the idea of being deceived by Satan? Are we too sophisticated or what? Explain.

READ

From *The Hidden Wound* by Wendell Berry[3]

Nine

To me, the great power that children possess is candor; they see the world clear eyed, without prejudice; honesty is not immediately conceived by them as an uncomfortable alternative to lying. On the contrary, the tactics of deceit are customarily given a high priority in the training of a child: "Don't say that in front of Aunt So-and-so." What we white Americans call manners and social conventions consist very largely of such tactics. A child is, as we say, impressionable, and acts directly on the basis of his experience. If a person is lovable or respectable, a child will love or respect him without first asking his class or his race or his income.

In a racist society, the candor of a child is therefore extremely threatening. That is also true of a puritanical society, as witness St. Paul, the genius of puritanism: "When I was a child, I spake as a child, I understood as a child, I thought as a child: but when I became a man I put away childish things." The crisis of life in both kinds of society is puberty, when the candor of childhood stands to be invested with sexual power, which would make it a threat both to current assumptions or pretensions, and to the survival of the same in future generations. The sexual man, possessed of a childlike clarity, threatens to *propagate* in the society the results of an elemental honesty which would be devastating. The puritan fears that it would bring about an awareness and a celebration of life in this world, the life of the senses, which would break the hold of the priesthood on the consciences and the purse strings of the populace. The racist fears that a child's honesty empowered by sex might turn in real and open affection toward members of the oppressed race, and so destroy the myth of the race's inferiority. This is perhaps why racism and puritanism have meshed so perfectly in the United States.

THINK   "I took all this in and thought it through, inside and out." (Ecclesiastes 9:1)

- In general, what do you think of Berry's words? Do you agree, disagree, feel confused, or what?
- What are some experiences you've had with the candor of a child? What about your own childhood—do you recall being coached to be deceitful under the guise of manners or social conventions? Explain.
- Berry believes that racism and puritanism have meshed nicely in the U.S. What do you think he means, and do you agree or disagree? Think this one through.

READ

From *To Kill a Mockingbird* by Harper Lee[4]

Just

(Scout Finch and her brother, Jem, have invited Walter Cunningham over to their house for dinner. Their father, Atticus, and the maid, Calpurnia, are both at the table as well. Walter is a country boy who doesn't wear shoes and has hookworms.)

While Walter piled food on his plate, he and Atticus talked together like two men, to the wonderment of Jem and me. Atticus was expounding upon farm problems when Walter interrupted to ask if there was any molasses in the house. Atticus summoned Calpurnia, who returned bearing the syrup pitcher. She stood waiting for Walter to help himself. Walter poured syrup on his vegetables and meat with a generous hand. He would probably have poured it into his milk glass had I not asked what the sam hill he was doing.

The silver saucer clattered when he replaced the pitcher, and he quickly put his hands in his lap. Then he ducked his head.

Atticus shook his head at me again. "But he's gone and drowned his dinner in syrup," I protested. "He's poured it all over."

It was then that Calpurnia requested my presence in the kitchen.

She was furious, and when she was furious Calpurnia's grammar became erratic. When in tranquility, her grammar was as good as anybody's in Maycomb. Atticus said Calpurnia had more education than most colored folks.

When she squinted down at me the tiny lines around her eyes deepened. "There's some folks who don't eat like us," she whispered fiercely, "but you ain't called on to contradict 'em at the table when they don't. That boy's yo' comp'ny and if he wants to eat up the table cloth you let him, you hear?"

"He ain't company, Cal, he's just a Cunningham."

"Hush your mouth! Don't matter who they are, anybody sets foot in this house's yo' comp'ny, and don't you let me catch you remarkin' on their ways like you was so high and mighty! Yo' folks might be better'n the Cunninghams but it don't count for nothin' the way you're disgracin' 'em—if you can't act fit to eat at the table you can just set here and eat in the kitchen!"

THINK   *"I took all this in and thought it through, inside and out."* (Ecclesiastes 9:1)

- "He ain't company, Cal, he's *just* a Cunningham" (emphasis added). Can you think of a time when you were in Walter's shoes? What happened, and what did you do? How about a time when you were in Scout's shoes?
- In either of those memories, did a "Calpurnia" intervene in some way for the good?
- Reread Colossians 3:9-11 at the beginning of this Letter. Paul writes, "From now on everyone is defined by Christ, everyone is included in Christ." How do you think those words mesh with Lee's story here?

PRAY

Slowly read the following poem a couple of times. What speaks to you? Ask God to bring a word or phrase to the surface. Then allow that word or phrase to begin your prayer. It might seem awkward at first. Fine, let it be awkward. But stick with it.

Genealogy

You are
in these hills
who you were and who you will become
and not just who you are
> She was a McKristy
> and his mother was a Smith
And the listeners nod
at what the combination will produce
those generations to come
of thievery or honesty
of heathens or Christians
of slovenly men or working
> 'Course her mother was a Sprayberry . . .

—JAMES A. AUTRY[5]

LIVE

These words from Autry serve as a reminder of this section's
theme—*lies*:

> You are . . .
> who you were and who you will become
> and not just who you are.

You've read from the journal entries, letters, and poems of
others. Now it's your turn. What does God want you to live when it
comes to *lies*? Use the space below to write a letter to yourself. You
might want to date the letter so you can reflect later where you were
and what was going on in your life regarding *lies*.

Date _____

Dear _____

"Regardless of what else you put on, wear love."
(COLOSSIANS 3:14)

Before You Begin

Take just a few moments to still your heart and mind. Remember, God desires to speak to *you* in these moments.

As high as heaven is over the earth,
so strong is his love to those who fear him.

PSALM 103:11

READ

Colossians 3:12-17

So, chosen by God for this new life of love, dress in the wardrobe God picked out for you: compassion, kindness, humility, quiet strength, discipline. Be even-tempered, content with second place, quick to forgive an offense. Forgive as quickly and completely as the Master forgave you. And regardless of what else you put on, wear love. It's your basic, all-purpose garment. Never be without it.

Let the peace of Christ keep you in tune with each other, in step with each other. None of this going off and doing your own thing. And cultivate thankfulness. Let the Word of Christ—the Message—have the run of the house. Give it plenty of room in your lives. Instruct and direct one another using good common sense. And sing, sing your hearts out to God! Let every detail in your lives—words, actions, whatever—be done in the name of the Master, Jesus, thanking God the Father every step of the way.

THINK

"I took all this in and thought it through, inside and out." (Ecclesiastes 9:1)

- Paul uses the imagery of getting dressed in this passage. In your own life, do you "put on" compassion, humility, quiet strength, and discipline each day, or do you reserve these qualities for special occasions?

- When you think of people who've offended you, are you usually "quick to forgive" the offense? If not, what holds you up? Explain.

- Do you usually wait until you see evidence of a changed life before offering forgiveness? If so, what's the rationale for that? How does that mesh with Paul's instructions here?

THINK (continued)

READ

From *Tuesdays with Morrie* by Mitch Albom[1]

Number Two

(The following is one of the entries from visits the author made to his dying professor, Morrie Schwartz.)

It is 1979, a basketball game in the Brandeis gym. The team is doing well, and the students section begins a chant, "We're number one! We're number one!" Morrie is sitting nearby. He is puzzled by the cheer. At one point, in the midst of "We're number one!" he rises and yells, "What's wrong with being number two?"

The students look at him. They stop chanting. He sits down, smiling and triumphant.

THINK

"I took all this in and thought it through, inside and out." (Ecclesiastes 9:1)

- Answer Morrie's question: "What's wrong with being number two?"
- In Colossians 3:12-17, Paul writes about being "content with second place." What do you think that means? How can you incorporate being number two into your daily life? Be as specific as you can.
- How does a "content with second place" mentality fit with striving for excellence, competition, leading to win, and all that?

READ

From *Community and Growth* by Jean Vanier[2]

Community as Forgiveness

We can only truly accept others as they are, and forgiven them, when we discover that we are truly accepted by God as we are and forgiven by him. It is a deep experience, knowing that we are loved and held by God in all our brokenness and littleness. . . . To accept responsibility for our sinfulness and hardness of heart, and to know that we are forgiven is a real liberation. I don't have to hide my guilt anymore.

We can only really love our enemies and all that is broken in them if we begin to love all that is broken in our own beings. The prodigal son, after the discovery that he was loved in such a tremendous way by the Father, would never be able to judge anyone any more. How could he reject someone when he sees how he had been accepted by the Father, just as he is, with all his brokenness. The elder son, on the other hand, did judge, because he had not come to terms with his own brokenness; all this was still hidden in the tomb of his being, with the stone rolled tight against it.

We can only really love with a universal heart as we discover that we are loved by the universal heart of God.

THINK "I took all this in and thought it through, inside and out." (Ecclesiastes 9:1)

- Do you have a personal context for the words "brokenness and littleness"? Explain.
- If you made a list of what's "broken" in your life right now, what are a few of the items topping your list? Have those areas recently been broken, or have they been on the fix-it list for a while?
- "Knowing that we are loved and held by God." What emotions do these words stir in you?

THINK (continued)

READ

From *The Romance of the Word* by Robert Farrar Capon[3]

Preface

(In Capon's view, a sacrament is not a transaction,
not an operation that produces an effect that wasn't there before.)

Take sacramental confession to a priest, for example. On its
surface, it looks for all the world like a transaction. A sinner,
foundering in her sins, comes to the confessional box. The
priest hears her sad tale of guilt and shame and then, with the
magic zap of absolution, sends her home pure as the driven
snow. But that won't wash. Every Sunday, in the Nicene Creed,
she proclaims her acknowledgement of "one baptism for the
forgiveness of sins." In her baptism, she was clothed with an
irremovable suit of forgiveness. All the sins she ever committed were committed inside that suit: she was forgiven before,
during, and after every last one of them. She does not "get"
forgiveness from the priest; rather, the priest pronounces over
her — really, authoritatively, *sacramentally* — the one forgiveness she already has. So it is indeed an absolution that she
receives; but it is not a new absolution, or a retreading of an
absolution that wore off — or, God forbid, a *handeling*, a bar-
gaining with God for an absolution she has to earn by proper
contrition. It's the same old free gift she never lost, but that she
has finally, by renewed faith, woken up to yet again. The priest's
words do indeed "convey" it to her faith in that dark box; but
she in no substantive way *acquires* it.

THINK   "I took all this in and thought it through, inside and
out." (Ecclesiastes 9:1)

- What thoughts or questions does this passage stir in you?
  How does it reflect or differ from your own experiences?
- "She does not 'get' forgiveness from the priest; rather, the
  priest pronounces over her . . . the one forgiveness she

already has." Do you agree with this statement? Why or why
not?

- How could this view of forgiveness affect the way you forgive
  others? Think this one through and ask your group for help.

READ

From *The Lord and His Prayer* by N. T. Wright[4]

Forgive Us Our Trespasses

(The "Running Father" in this excerpt describes the prodigal son's father, who saw his son from a distance and ran to greet him in Luke 15.)

Only when we understand why this man is running will we really understand what Jesus meant when he taught us to pray: Forgive us our trespasses, as we forgive those who trespass against us.

We need shocking stories like the Running Father, because our generation has either forgotten about forgiveness or trivialized it. Once you replace morality with the philosophy that says "if it feels good, do it," there isn't anything to forgive; if you still feel hurt by something, our culture suggests that you should simply retreat into your private world and pretend it didn't happen. In that sort of world, I don't need God to forgive me, and I don't need to forgive anybody else, either. Or, if people do still think about forgiveness, they seldom get beyond the small-scale private forgiveness of small-scale private sins. They hope God will forgive their peccadillos, and they try at least to smile benignly on their neighbours' follies.

Instead of genuine forgiveness, our generation has been taught the vague notion of "tolerance." This is, at best, a low-grade parody of forgiveness. . . . If the Father in the story had intended merely to *tolerate* the son, he would not have been running down the road to meet him. Forgiveness is richer and higher and harder and more shocking than we usually think. Jesus' message offers the genuine article, and insists that we should accept no man-made substitutes.

THINK   "I took all this in and thought it through, inside and out." (Ecclesiastes 9:1)

- "Instead of genuine forgiveness, our generation has been taught the vague notion of 'tolerance.'" What do you think of this statement? Do you find it true in your life or not? Explain.

- "Forgiveness is richer and higher and harder and more shocking than we usually think." Do you think this statement is true or false? Defend your answer.

- Do you think most Christians merely tolerate one another? In Colossians 3:13, Paul writes, "Forgive . . . quickly and completely." Can "tolerate" ever be the same as "forgive . . . quickly"? Why or why not?

PRAY

Slowly read the following poem a couple of times. What speaks to you? Ask God to bring a word or phrase to the surface. Then allow that word or phrase to begin your prayer. It might seem awkward at first. Fine, let it be awkward. But stick with it.

This Is Just to Say

I have eaten
the plums
that were in
the icebox

and which
you were probably
saving
for breakfast

Forgive me
they were delicious
so sweet
and so cold.

— WILLIAM CARLOS WILLIAMS[5]

LIVE

These words from Williams serve as a reminder of this section's theme—*love*:

Forgive me.

You've read from the journal entries, letters, and poems of others. Now it's your turn. What does God want you to live when it comes to *love*? Use the space below to write a letter to yourself. You might want to date the letter so you can reflect later where you were and what was going on in your life regarding *love*.

Date _____

Dear _____

FAMILY

"Do your best. Work from the heart for your real Master."
(Colossians 3:22)

Before You Begin

Take just a few moments to still your heart and mind. Remember, God desires to speak to *you* in these moments.

> *If God hadn't been there for me,*
> *I never would have made it.*
>
> PSALM 94:17

READ

Colossians 3:18-25

Wives, understand and support your husbands by submitting to them in ways that honor the Master.

Husbands, go all out in love for your wives. Don't take advantage of them.

Children, do what your parents tell you. This delights the Master no end.

Parents, don't come down too hard on your children or you'll crush their spirits.

Servants, do what you're told by your earthly masters. And don't just do the minimum that will get you by. Do your best. Work from the heart for your real Master, for God, confident that you'll get paid in full when you come into your inheritance. Keep in mind always that the ultimate Master you're serving is Christ. The sullen servant who does shoddy work will be held responsible. Being a follower of Jesus doesn't cover up bad work.

THINK

"I took all this in and thought it through, inside and out." (Ecclesiastes 9:1)

- What's your response to these verses? Do they speak to you at all? Paul usually isn't afraid of using plenty of words to make his point, so why do you think he wrote in such a bulleted-list style here?
- Would you characterize your normal workday as "work from the heart"? Why or why not?
- What about your relationships with family—do you approach those with the same value as your relationship with the "real Master"? More value? Less value? Explain.

THINK (continued)

READ

From *The Proper Care and Feeding of Husbands* by Dr. Laura Schlessinger[1]

Introduction

"I am a thirty-seven-year-old man who has seen quite a bit in life, and I can offer this to your search for how to treat a man. We are men, not dumb-dumbs, psychics, or one bit unromantic. We need only clear communication, appreciation, honest love, and respect. This will be repaid by laying the moon and stars at your feet for your pleasure. There is no need to 'work' a man to get what you want. We live to take care of a wife, family, and home. Just remember that we are men, and know that our needs are simple but not *to be* ignored. A good man is hard to find, not to keep."

—Dan

THINK   "I took all this in and thought it through, inside and out." (Ecclesiastes 9:1)

- "A good man is hard to find, not to keep." Dr. Laura used that sentence as the springboard for her book. What do you think of this statement as a foundation for the marital relationship?
- How do Dan's words stack up with Paul's brief commands to wives and husbands?

READ

From *If Only He Knew* by Gary Smalley[2]

Serious Consequences

First, a woman who is not properly loved by her husband can develop any number of serious physical ailments needing thousands of dollars' worth of treatment. . . .

Second, every aspect of a woman's emotional and physical existence is dependent on the romantic love she receives from her husband. . . . So, husbands, if you feel locked out of your bedroom, listen closely. . . .

Third, a husband's lack of love for his wife can drastically affect their children's emotional development. . . .

Fourth, a disrespectful wife and rebellious children are more likely to be found in the home of a man who does not know how to lovingly support his family.

THINK   "I took all this in and thought it through, inside and out." (Ecclesiastes 9:1)

- If you're a husband, how do you react to Smalley's words?
- If you're a wife, do you think Smalley speaks truth here? Anything you're not sure about?
- Paul writes to husbands, "Go all out in love for your wives" (Colossians 3:19). Do you think following Paul's command would take care of the problems on Smalley's list? Explain.

THINK (continued)

READ

From *The Child's Song* by Donald Capps[3]

The Mutilated Soul

(Here Capps refers to Alice Miller's book *For Your Own Good*. For more than twenty-five years, Alice Miller has been speaking out against child abuse.)

Miller is especially concerned in *For Your Own Good* with child-rearing theories and methods that have proved effective in crushing the spontaneous feelings of children. These theories and methods address the fact that those concerned with raising children have often had difficulty dealing with the child's obstinancy, willfulness, and defiance and with the exuberant character of children's emotions. The poisonous pedagogies that Miller reviews in her book are largely concerned with advising parents on how to break the will of the child, and doing this without emotion (e.g., anger). By acting without emotion, the parent expects the child to react similarly. If the child persists in responding emotionally to a spanking or other reprimand, by getting angry or by crying, the parent threatens the child with another spanking. The goal is to eliminate feeling from the act of punishment and from the child's response to it.

Childrearing theorists also point out to parents that if they are successful in containing their own emotions, they thereby communicate to the child that they are not acting in their own interests, but in the interests of the child. They are punishing the child for the child's "own good." Thus, it is anticipated that the child, rather than being resentful of the punishment, will come to be grateful for it, and may even come to believe that the punishment is an expression of the parent's love for the child: "I would not hurt you if I did not love you." Children who learn to be grateful for the punishment they received as children will inflict the same punishment on their own children since not to do so would be an indication of their lack of interest, concern, and even love for the child.

THINK   "I took all this in and thought it through, inside and out." (Ecclesiastes 9:1)

- Consider your childhood. What feelings do Miller's words bring to the surface? Spend some time on this.
- What about your children? Grandchildren? Nephews and nieces? Do you see their spirits being crushed? Are you one of the "crushers"?

READ

From *Never Mind the Joneses* by Tim Stafford[4]

The Struggle to Find Grace

When I lie awake at night, my thoughts easily fall into a rant of bitterness or regret. Fears and recriminations boil up. I find anxious thoughts hard to lay aside. I have to work hard to pray with thanksgiving and love.

No wonder that in the daylight I find it hard to react graciously to someone who wrongs me . . . or that I can react punitively or sarcastically when my kids make a mistake. I need grace. I can offer to others only what I possess, and grace is not a constant in my life.

We cannot make ourselves gracious. Grace comes from heaven. We cannot manufacture it, no matter how hard we try. . . .

Not only will God always give grace to those willing to accept it, he has tied that grace to a place we can find. We do not search for grace in dark spiritual mysteries. Grace has come to earth in Jesus; grace has come to earth in his body, the church. Grace is available for us and for our families.

THINK

"I took all this in and thought it through, inside and out." (Ecclesiastes 9:1)

- If you have children, can you recall the last time you acted graciously toward them? Did you "manufacture" some sort of cheap imitation grace? Or could you offer grace "from heaven"?
- Stafford writes, "Grace has come to earth in Jesus; grace has come to earth in his body, the church." When you think of what you call a church family—a small group, house church, or traditional congregation—does it seem like a place where you experience and learn grace? Elaborate.

THINK (continued)

PRAY

Slowly read the following poem a couple of times. What speaks to you? Ask God to bring a word or phrase to the surface. Then allow that word or phrase to begin your prayer. It might seem awkward at first. Fine, let it be awkward. But stick with it.

First Lesson

Lie back, daughter, let your head
be tipped back in the cup of my hand.
Gently, and I will hold you. Spread
your arms wide, lie out on the stream
and look high at the gulls. A dead-
man's-float is face down. You will dive
and swim soon enough where this tidewater
ebbs to the sea. Daughter, believe
me, when you tire on the long thrash
to your island, lie up, and survive.
As you float now, where I held you
and let go, remember when fear
cramps your heart what I told you:
lie gently and wide to the light-year
stars, lie back, and the sea will hold you.

— PHILIP BOOTH[5]

LIVE

These words from Booth serve as a reminder of this section's theme—*family*:

> let your head
> be tipped back in the cup of my hand.
> Gently, and I will hold you.

You've read from the journal entries, letters, and poems of others. Now it's your turn. What does God want you to live when it comes to *family*? Use the space below to write a letter to yourself. You might want to date the letter so you can reflect later where you were and what was going on in your life regarding *family*.

Date _____

Dear _____

PRAYER

"Pray diligently. Stay alert, with your eyes wide open in gratitude." (Colossians 4:2)

Before You Begin

Take just a few moments to still your heart and mind. Remember, God desires to speak to *you* in these moments.

> *The revelation of God is whole*
> *and pulls our lives together.*
>
> PSALM 19:7

READ

Colossians 4:1-6

Masters, treat your servants considerately. Be fair with them. Don't forget for a minute that you, too, serve a Master—God in heaven.

Pray diligently. Stay alert, with your eyes wide open in gratitude. Don't forget to pray for us, that God will open doors for telling the mystery of Christ, even while I'm locked up in this jail. Pray that every time I open my mouth I'll be able to make Christ plain as day to them.

Use your heads as you live and work among outsiders. Don't miss a trick. Make the most of every opportunity. Be gracious in your speech. The goal is to bring out the best in others in a conversation, not put them down, not cut them out.

THINK   *"I took all this in and thought it through, inside and out."* (Ecclesiastes 9:1)

- Do you ever pray with your "eyes wide open"? Do you think it matters how we pray?
- Paul writes, "Don't miss a trick. Make the most of every opportunity." How does that sound to you? What do you think he means?

READ

From *Working the Angles* by Eugene Peterson[1]

Praying by the Book

That is why so many of the old masters counsel caution: Be slow to pray. This is not an enterprise to be entered into lightly. When we pray we are using words that bring us into proximity with words that break cedars, shake the wilderness, make the oaks whirl, and strip forests bare (Ps. 29:5-9). When we pray we use words that may well leave us quavering, soul-shattered, on our faces: "Woe is me! For I am lost; for I am a man of unclean lips . . . !" (Isa. 6:5). When we pray we have a more than average chance of ending up in a place that we quite definitely never wanted to be, angrily protesting, preferring death to the kind of life that God insists on recklessly throwing us into: "O Lord, take my life from me, I beseech thee, for it is better for me to die than to live" (Jon. 4:3). We want life on our conditions, not on God's conditions. Praying puts us at risk of getting involved in God's conditions. Be slow to pray.

THINK   "I took all this in and thought it through, inside and out." (Ecclesiastes 9:1)

- Has anyone ever urged you to "be slow to pray"? How did you react? How does that statement make you respond now?
- Peterson writes, "Praying puts us at risk of getting involved in God's conditions." In your own words, what do you think that means? Describe a time when you realized the truth of this statement. Be specific.

THINK (continued)

READ

From *Pilgrim at Tinker Creek* by Annie Dillard[2]

Seeing

Seeing is of course very much a matter of verbalization. Unless I call my attention to what passes before my eyes, I simply won't see it. It is, as Ruskin says, "not merely unnoticed, but in the full, clear sense of the word, unseen." My eyes alone can't solve analogy tests without figures, the ones which show, with increasing elaborations, a big square, then a small square in a big square, then a big triangle, and expect me to find a small triangle in a big triangle. I have to say the words, describe what I'm seeing.

THINK

"I took all this in and thought it through, inside and out." (Ecclesiastes 9:1)

- Dillard writes, "I have to say the words, describe what I'm seeing." Use this statement as a guide and pray right now. "With your eyes wide open in gratitude" (Colossians 4:2), describe what you see.
- How did that feel? Did it seem like a prayer or not? Do you think God heard it as a prayer?

READ

From *The Contemplative Pastor* by Eugene Peterson[3]

Praying with Eyes Open

Matter is real. Flesh is good. Without a firm rooting in creation, religion is always drifting off into some kind of pious sentimentalism or sophisticated intellectualism. The task of salvation is not to refine us into pure spirits so that we will not be cumbered with this too solid flesh. We are not angels, nor are we to become angels. The Word did not become a good idea, or a numinous feeling, or a moral aspiration; the Word became flesh. It also becomes flesh. Our Lord left us a command to remember and receive him in bread and wine, in acts of eating and drinking. Things matter. The physical is holy. It is extremely significant that in the opening sentences of the Bible, God speaks a world of energy and matter into being. . . . Apart from creation, covenant has no structure, no context, no rootage in reality.

THINK   "I took all this in and thought it through, inside and out." (Ecclesiastes 9:1)

- When you opened your eyes and prayed after Dillard's reading, what did you see? Matter? Flesh? Creation?
- A lot of preachers and teachers refer to human flesh as evil and only spiritual matters as holy. Peterson writes that "flesh is good." What do you think he means? Do you agree or not? Explain.

THINK (continued)

READ

From *No Holds Barred* by Mark Roberts[4]

Savoring Life Through Thanksgiving

Taking life for granted is one of our most common bad habits. Usually we don't realize how much we do this until an unexpected event alters our perspective and surprises us with the gift of gratitude. I discovered this truth during my first Thanksgiving vacation as a college freshman. In September 1975 I left California to enter college in Massachusetts. For the next seventy-five days, I lived in a freshman dorm, a rather Spartan existence, but not an unpleasant one.

Since I couldn't afford to go home for Thanksgiving, I traveled by bus to central Connecticut to join some family friends for the holiday. On Thanksgiving Eve, as I retired to my room, I slipped off my shoes and socks to unpack my bags. I felt the carpet under my bare feet, enjoying the softness and the feel of the threads between my toes. Suddenly it dawned on me that I hadn't felt carpet like this since I'd left home. . . .

How could something so ordinary feel so enjoyable? I wondered what else I'd been taking for granted. That weekend in Connecticut added several other items to my list of newly discovered appreciation, including ceramic mugs, quiet nights, and a bathroom heater. . . .

If you want to experience life in all its fullness, take time to thank the Lord more often. Offer thanks for things big and small, for the usual as well as the unique.

THINK "I took all this in and thought it through, inside and out." (Ecclesiastes 9:1)

- In the previous reading, Peterson writes, "The physical is holy." Here, Roberts writes, "I wondered what else I'd been taking for granted." Do you think God really cares if we appreciate the mundane things of life?
- Do you find it easy to offer gratitude for "things big and small, for the usual as well as the unique"? Explain.

PRAY

Slowly read the following poem a couple of times. What speaks to you? Ask God to bring a word or phrase to the surface. Then allow that word or phrase to begin your prayer. It might seem awkward at first. Fine, let it be awkward. But stick with it.

&

Blessed Are Those Who Mourn

Flash floods of tears, torrents of them,
Erode cruel canyons, exposing
Long forgotten strata of life
Laid down in the peaceful decades:
A badlands beauty. The same sun
That decorates each day with colors
From arroyos and mesas, also shows
Every old scar and cut of lament.
Weeping washes the wounds clean
And leaves them to heal, which always
Takes an age or two. No pain
Is ugly in past tense. Under
The Mercy every hurt is a fossil
Link in the great chain of becoming.
Pick and shovel prayers often
Turn them up in the valleys of death.

— EUGENE PETERSON[5]

LIVE

These words serve as a reminder of this section's theme—*prayer*:

Pick and shovel prayers often
Turn them up in the valleys of death.

You've read from the journal entries, letters, and poems of others. Now it's your turn. What does God want you to live when it comes to *prayer*? Use the space below to write a letter to yourself. You might want to date the letter so you can reflect later where you were and what was going on in your life regarding *prayer*.

Date _____

Dear _____

NO RULES, JUST WRITE

"Remember to pray for me in this jail. Grace be with you."
(Colossians 4:18)

Before You Begin

Take just a few moments to still your heart and mind. Remember, God desires to speak to *you* in these moments.

> *I'm ready to offer the thanksgiving sacrifice*
> *and pray in the name of God.*
>
> PSALM 116:17

READ

Colossians 4:7-18

My good friend Tychicus will tell you all about me. He's a trusted minister and companion in the service of the Master. I've sent him to you so that you would know how things are with us, and so he could encourage you in your faith. And I've sent Onesimus with him. Onesimus is one of you, and has become such a trusted and dear brother! Together they'll bring you up-to-date on everything that has been going on here.

Aristarchus, who is in jail here with me, sends greetings; also Mark, cousin of Barnabas (you received a letter regarding him; if he shows up, welcome him); and also Jesus, the one they call Justus. These are the only ones left from the old crowd who have stuck with me in working for God's kingdom. Don't think they haven't been a big help!

Epaphras, who is one of you, says hello. What a trooper he has been! He's been tireless in his prayers for you, praying that you'll stand firm, mature and confident in everything God wants you to do. I've watched him closely, and can report on how hard he has worked for you and for those in Laodicea and Hierapolis.

Luke, good friend and physician, and Demas both send greetings.

Say hello to our friends in Laodicea; also to Nympha and the church that meets in her house.

After this letter has been read to you, make sure it gets read also in Laodicea. And get the letter that went to Laodicea and have it read to you.

And, oh, yes, tell Archippus, "Do your best in the job you received from the Master. Do your very best."

I'm signing off in my own handwriting—Paul. Remember to pray for me in this jail. Grace be with you.

You've walked through Paul's letter to the Colossians. You've also walked through journal entries, letters, and poems from other pilgrims along the way. Now it's your turn. The challenge before you is to write three letters to three friends. These could include your spouse, an uncle you haven't spoken to for years, a former teacher, or your best friend from grade school. Go back through the lessons and allow God's Spirit to remind you of particularly meaningful places in Colossians, journal entries that resonated with you, or poems that touched you deeply. Then allow time for the faces of those family or friends to surface alongside those words.

Give this some time. If you build the space, they will come.

Just a side note: You don't have to limit your recipients to those who are living. You might write a letter to a grandparent who passed away or a soldier who died in harm's way. At times, writing to those who have gone on can open the door to significant growth and healing in our lives.

Then sit down with paper and pencil, or keyboard and screen, and share some of the thoughts and feelings that come to the surface. This might seem to be an unorthodox way to finish. But remember, this isn't a Bible study. The letters you send carry the possibility of witness, a way to invite soulfulness in a soul-less world. May they prompt reflection in another heart, honor the always-appropriate gift of memory, and speak truths of the past into today and eternity.

\ \ \ \

As you begin your letters (but end this book), ground your intentions by filling in three names.

Dear _____.

Dear _____.

Dear _____.

NOTES

LETTER 1: **STALWART**

1. *Dictionary.com*, s.v. "stalwart," http://dictionary reference.com/browse/stalwart (accessed May 29, 2007).
2. Robert Falcon Scott, *Scott's Last Expedition: The Journals* (New York: Carroll & Graf Publishers, 1996), 388–389.
3. Apsley Cherry-Garrard, *The Worst Journey in the World* (New York: Carroll & Graf Publishers, 1989), 643.
4. Barry Lopez, *Arctic Dreams: Imagination and Desire in a Northern Landscape* (New York: Bantam Books, 1987), 308–309.
5. Frederick Buechner, *Brendan: A Novel* (New York: HarperSanFrancisco, 1988), 3–6.
6. T. E. Lawrence, "The Seven Pillars of Wisdom," in Joe Simpson, *Touching the Void* (New York: HarperPerennial, 1988), title page.

LETTER 2: **INCARNATION**

1. Don Everts, *God in the Flesh: What Speechless Lawyers, Kneeling Soldiers and Shocked Crowds Teach Us About Jesus* (Downers Grove, IL: InterVarsity, 2005), 14–15.
2. M. Scott Peck, *Further Along the Road Less Traveled*, quoted in Philip Yancey, *The Jesus I Never Knew* (Grand Rapids, MI: Zondervan, 1995), 257.
3. Lauren F. Winner, *Girl Meets God: On the Path to a Spiritual Life* (New York: Shaw Books, 2004), 73–74. Reprinted from *Girl Meets God*. Copyright © 2002 by Lauren F. Winner. Used by permission of WaterBrook Press, Colorado Springs, CO. All rights reserved.
4. Frederick Buechner, *The Magnificent Defeat* (San Francisco: Harper & Row, 1966), 47–48.

5. Eugene Peterson, "The Dream," in *The Contemplative Pastor: Returning to the Art of Spiritual Direction* (Grand Rapids, MI: Wm. B. Eerdmans Publishing Company, 1989), 163. Reprinted by permission of the author and publisher; all rights reserved.

LETTER 3: **SUFFERING**

1. Nicholas Wolterstorff, *Lament for a Son* (Grand Rapids, MI: Eerdmans, 1987), 90.
2. Annie Dillard, *For the Time Being* (New York: Vintage Books, 1999), 84–85.
3. Excerpt from pages 142–144 from *Ragman and Other Cries of Faith* by Walter Wangerin Jr. Copyright © 1984 by Walter Wangerin Jr. Reprinted by permission of HarperCollins Publishers.
4. Selection from pages 66–67 from *The Hungering Dark* by Frederick Buechner. Copyright © 1969 by Frederick Buechner. Reprinted by permission of HarperCollins Publishers.
5. Lamentations 3:19-24.

LETTER 4: **LIVING**

1. Christoph Blumhardt, *Action in Waiting* (Farmington, PA: The Plough Publishing House, 1998), 74–75.
2. Brent Curtis and John Eldredge, *The Sacred Romance: Drawing Closer to the Heart of God* (Nashville: Nelson, 1997), 136–137.
3. Ken Gire, *Intimate Moments with the Savior: Learning to Love* (Grand Rapids, MI: Zondervan, 1989), 66–67.
4. Brennan Manning, *Abba's Child: The Cry of the Heart for Intimate Belonging* (Colorado Springs, CO: NavPress, 1994), 51–53.
5. Denise Levertov, "Living," in *Poems 1960–1967* (New York: New Directions Publishing Corp., 1966), 240. Permission pending.

LETTER 5: **GRACE**

1. David James Duncan, *The River Why* (New York: Sierra Club Books, 1983), 14–15.

2. "Protestant," from *Lake Wobegon Days* by Garrison Keillor, copyright © 1985 by Garrison Keillor, 107–108. Used by permission of Viking Penguin, a division of Penguin Group (USA) Inc.

3. John Eldredge, *Waking the Dead: The Glory of a Heart Fully Alive* (Nashville: Nelson, 2003), 105.

4. Robert Farrar Capon, *Between Noon and Three: Romance, Law, and the Outrage of Grace* (Grand Rapids, MI: Eerdmans, 1997), 109.

5. James Kavanaugh, "I Don't Pray So Very Well," in *Tears and Laughter of a Man's Soul* (Highland Park, IL: Steven J. Nash, 1990), 110. Permission pending.

LETTER 6: **CHOICE**

1. Taken from *The Jesus I Never Knew* by Philip D. Yancey. Copyright © 1995 by Philip Yancey, 153. Used by permission of Zondervan.

2. Madeleine L'Engle, *Walking on Water: Reflections on Faith and Art* (Wheaton, IL: Harold Shaw Publishers, 1980), 103–104.

3. E. B. White, *Charlotte's Web*, in *A Call to Character*, Colin Green and Herbert Kohl, eds. (New York: HarperCollins, 1995), 31. Permission pending.

4. Richard Bach, *Jonathan Livingston Seagull: A Story* (New York: The Macmillian Company, 1970), 35–36.

5. Mary Oliver, "Just As the Calendar Began to Say Summer," in *Long Life: Essays and Other Writings* (Cambridge, MA: Da Capo Press, 2004), 35. Reprinted by permission of Da Capo Press, a member of the Perseus Books Group.

LETTER 7: **REAL LIFE**

1. Lynda Sexson, *Ordinarily Sacred* (Charlottesville: University Press of Virginia, 1992), 3.

2. Frederick Buechner, *The Alphabet of Grace* (New York: HarperCollins, 1970), 34–35.

3. Gerald May, *The Awakened Heart: Opening Yourself to the Love You Need* (New York: HarperCollins, 1991), 31.

4. Norman Maclean, *A River Runs Through It* (Chicago: The University of Chicago Press, 1976), 20–22. © 1976 by The University of Chicago. All rights reserved.

5. David Budbill, "Dilemma" from *Moment to Moment: Poems of a Mountain Recluse*. Copyright © 1999 by David Budbill. Reprinted with the permission of Copper Canyon Press, www.coppercanyonpress.org.

LETTER 8: **LIES**

1. M. Scott Peck, *People of the Lie: The Hope for Healing Human Evil* (New York: Touchstone, 1983), 207.

2. John Eldredge, *Wild at Heart: Discovering the Passionate Soul of a Man* (Nashville: Nelson, 2001), 152–153.

3. Excerpt from *The Hidden Wound* by Wendell Berry. Copyright © 1989 by Wendell Berry. Reprinted by permission of North Point Press, a division of Farrar, Straus and Giroux, LLC.

4. Excerpt from pages 30–31 from *To Kill a Mockingbird* by Harper Lee. Copyright © 1960 by Harper Lee; renewed 1988 by Harper Lee. Foreword copyright © 1993 by Harper Lee. Reprinted by permission of HarperCollins Publishers.

5. James A. Autry, "Genealogy," in Bill Moyers, *The Language of Life: A Festival of Poets*, ed. James Haba (New York: Doubleday, 1995), 17–19.

LETTER 9: **LOVE**

1. Mitch Albom, *Tuesdays with Morrie: An Old Man, a Young Man, and Life's Greatest Lesson* (New York: Doubleday, 1997), 159.

2. Jean Vanier, *Community and Growth* (New York: Paulist, 1979), 36–37.

3. Robert Farrar Capon, *The Romance of the Word: One Man's Love Affair with Theology* (Grand Rapids, MI: Eerdmans, 1995), 23–24.

4. N. T. Wright, *The Lord and His Prayer* (Grand Rapids, MI: Eerdmans, 1996), 50–51.

5. "This Is Just to Say," by William Carlos Williams, from *The Collected Poems of William Carlos Williams: 1909–1939*, Volume 1, 372, copyright © 1938 by New Directions Publishing Corp. Reprinted 1991. Reprinted by permission of New Directions Publishing Corp.

LETTER 10: FAMILY

1. Dr. Laura Schlessinger, *The Proper Care and Feeding of Husbands* (New York: HarperCollins, 2004), xiii.
2. Gary Smalley, *If Only He Knew: Understanding Your Wife* (Grand Rapids, MI: Zondervan, 1979), 17–18.
3. Donald Capps, *The Child's Song: The Religious Abuse of Children* (Louisville, KY: Westminster John Knox, 1995), 7.
4. Tim Stafford, *Never Mind the Joneses: Building Core Christian Values in a Way That Fits Your Family* (Downers Grove, IL: InterVarsity, 2004), 201–202.
5. "First Lesson," from *Lifelines: Selected Poems 1950–1999* by Philip Booth, copyright © 1999 by Philip Booth. Used by permission of Viking Penguin, a division of Penguin Group (USA) Inc.

LETTER 11: PRAYER

1. Eugene Peterson, *Working the Angles: The Shape of Pastoral Integrity* (Grand Rapids, MI: Eerdmans, 1987), 43–44.
2. Annie Dillard, *Pilgrim at Tinker Creek* (New York: HarperPerennial, 1974), 30–31.
3. Eugene Peterson, *The Contemplative Pastor: Returning to the Art of Spiritual Direction* (Grand Rapids, MI: Eerdmans, 1989), 68.
4. Mark Roberts, *No Holds Barred: Wrestling with God in Prayer* (Colorado Springs, CO: WaterBrook, 2005), 118–119.
5. Eugene Peterson, "Blessed Are Those Who Mourn," in *The Contemplative Pastor: Returning to the Art of Spiritual Direction* (Grand Rapids, MI: Wm. B. Eerdmans Publishing Company, 1989), 67. Reprinted by permission of the author and publisher; all rights reserved.

CHECK OUT THESE OTHER GREAT TITLES FROM THE Living the Letters SERIES!

In a modern world filled with disposable e-mails, receiving a handwritten letter remains one of life's simple pleasures. Rediscover the power of the written word through Paul's insightful letters.

Living the Letters: Galatians
The Navigators
978-1-60006-029-8
1-60006-029-3

Explore the rich wisdom of Galatians on topics such as spiritual discernment, intimacy with God, and our freedom in Christ.

Living the Letters: Ephesians
The Navigators
978-1-60006-030-4
1-60006-030-7

Paul writes to the Ephesians about finding your identity in Christ, experiencing the fullness of God, and living with faithful abandon.

Living the Letters: Philippians
The Navigators
978-1-60006-161-5
1-60006-161-3

Gain valuable insight from Paul's letter to the Philippians about proclaiming Christ, loving well, and celebrating God.